The Night Wilt Scored 100

Also by Eric Nadel

The Man Who Stole First Base (*with Craig R. Wright*)

The Night Wilt Scored 100

Tales From Basketball's Past

by
Eric Nadel

Taylor Publishing Company
Dallas, Texas

Published by Taylor Publishing Company
1550 West Mockingbird Lane
Dallas, Texas 75235

Designed by Robert Krug

Photo credits appear on page 175.

Library of Congress Cataloging-in-Publication Data

Nadel, Eric
The night Wilt scored 100 : tales from basketball's past / Eric Nadel.
p. cm.
ISBN 0-87833-662-1 : $9.95
1. Basketball—History—Miscellanea. I. Title. II. Title: Night Wilt scored one hundred.
GV883.N33 1990
796.323'09—dc20 90-34641
CIP

Printed in the United States of America

10 9 8 7 6 5 4 3 2 1

To the memory of my father, and to my mother.
Their understanding and encouragement of my
passion for sports made it possible for
me to live out my dream.

Introduction

I'll never forget my first exposure to pro basketball—a Sunday afternoon subway ride in 1961 from Brooklyn to Manhattan to watch Wilt Chamberlain and the Harlem Globetrotters from court-side seats at Madison Square Garden. My father had told me the story of the 7′1″ giant who had left Kansas University to join the Globetrotters. But nothing could prepare a nine-year-old for his first view of a human being that large, or the experience of witnessing the magic performed by Wilt and his teammates that afternoon.

Nor was I in any way ready for the sight that followed during the warm-ups for the second game, an NBA contest between the Knicks and the Syracuse Nationals. When the teams hit the floor, I couldn't believe my eyes as out thundered a man even taller and wider than Wilt himself. This man-mountain was Syracuse center Swede Halbrook, who was listed in my program as 7′3″, but who appeared to be at least a foot taller than that.

Halbrook played only two years in the NBA, but he would be forever etched in my memory if he had never played another game. And yet, whenever I bring up his name to my contemporaries, I am met with vacant stares.

While working on *The Man Who Stole First Base—Tales From Baseball's Past,* co-author Craig Wright and I sought out material about players and events that even the most avid baseball fans had never heard of, as well as generally unknown stories about well-known heroes. In the process, I realized that to basketball fans, virtually nothing in the past is familiar. Basketball lore has somehow failed to make its way into the consciousness of the huge and growing legion of basketball followers.

Why does everyone know so much about Babe Ruth and the Yankee dynasty of the '20s, and so little about George Mikan and the Laker dynasty of the '40s and early '50s?

Why can anyone tell you who Jackie Robinson is, while even a die-hard basketball fan cannot identify Chuck Cooper, a man of similar status?

And why has Shoeless Joe Jackson become a cult figure of huge proportions, while the average NBA follower has never heard of Alex Groza?

Basketball has its legends, too, dating all the way back to James Naismith, who thought he was inventing a game that could be played by eighty people at a time. There was Hank Luisetti, whose introduction of the jump shot revolutionized the game; Bevo Francis, who scored over one hundred points in a college game not once but twice; and Danny Biasone, whose ingenious suggestion saved the game of pro basketball.

There were blind dribblers and blindfolded free throw shooters, teams that won hundreds of games in a row, and games played on horseback and on roller skates.

And of course, there were the two giants who had captivated my nine-year-old attention span. Just finding out more about Swede Halbrook, "The World's Tallest Basketball Player," made this project worthwhile for me. And reliving the night Wilt scored 100 resurrected all my initial wonderment in witnessing the greatest scoring machine in basketball history.

Perhaps this book can be considered my humble contribution to the acceptance of basketball lore. The heroes found on these pages certainly deserve the recognition. I hope you'll find their stories as intriguing and entertaining as I did.

The Night Wilt Scored 100

On December 8, 1961, 7′1″ Wilt Chamberlain scored 78 points for the Philadelphia Warriors in a triple-overtime game. It was a new NBA record, but Warriors coach Frank McGuire didn't expect it to last long, saying, "He'll get 100 points someday."

McGuire's prediction came true just a few months later in a game against the New York Knicks at Hershey, Pennsylvania, where the Warriors played a few games each year. A crowd of 4,124 turned out on March 2, 1962, partially to see a preliminary game between players from two NFL teams, the Philadelphia Eagles and Baltimore Colts. But what they'd remember was the greatest individual scoring achievement in NBA history.

The Knicks' regular center, Phil Jordan, was out with the flu, and 6′11″ Darrall Imhoff, who was known for his rugged defense, started in the middle. "Wilt the Stilt" poured in 23 points in the first quarter, as Imhoff quickly got into foul

PHILADELPHIA WARRIORS (169)

Player	Pos.	Min.	FGA	FGM	FTA	FTM	Reb.	Ast.	PF	Pts.
Paul Arizin	F	31	18	7	2	2	5	4	0	16
Ed Conlin		14	4	0	0	0	4	1	1	0
Joe Ruklick		8	1	0	2	0	2	1	2	0
Tom Meschery	F	40	12	7	2	2	7	3	4	16
Ted Luckenbill		3	0	0	0	0	1	0	2	0
Wilt Chamberlain	C	48	63	36	32	28	25	2	2	100
Guy Rodgers	G	48	4	1	12	9	7	20	5	11
Al Attles	G	34	8	8	1	1	5	6	4	17
York Larese		14	5	4	1	1	1	2	5	9
Totals		240	115	63	52	43	60	39	25	169

Team Rebounds—3.

NEW YORK KNICKS (147)

Player	Pos.	Min.	FGA	FGM	FTA	FTM	Reb.	Ast.	PF	Pts.
Willie Naulls	F	43	22	9	15	13	7	2	5	31
Johnny Green	F	21	7	3	0	0	7	1	5	6
Cleveland Buckner		33	26	16	1	1	8	0	4	33
Darrall Imhoff	C	20	7	3	1	1	6	0	6	7
Dave Budd		27	8	6	1	1	10	1	1	13
Richie Guerin	G	46	29	13	17	13	8	6	5	39
Al Butler	G	32	13	4	0	0	7	3	1	8
Donnie Butcher		18	6	3	6	4	3	4	5	10
Totals		240	118	57	41	33	60	17	32	147

Team Rebounds—4.

Score by Periods:	1st	2nd	3rd	4th	Totals
Philadelphia	42	37	46	44	— 169
New York	26	42	38	41	— 147

CHAMBERLAIN'S SCORING BY PERIODS

	Min.	FGA	FGM	FTA	FTM	Reb.	Ast.	PF	Pts.
First Quarter	12	14	7	9	9	10	0	0	23
Second Quarter	12	12	7	5	4	4	1	1	18
Third Quarter	12	16	10	8	8	6	1	0	28
Fourth Quarter	12	21	12	10	7	5	0	1	31
Totals	48	63	36	32	28	25	2	2	100

Referees—Willie Smith and Pete D'Ambrosio. Attendance—4,124.

trouble. Protesting one of those calls, Imhoff complained to the referee, "Why don't you just give him 100 points and we'll go home!" Little did he know how prophetic that statement would be.

Hitting on fadeaways, finger rolls, and dunks, Wilt added 18 in the second quarter, playing mostly against 6′9″ forward Cleveland Buckner, to finish the first half with 41. Wilt finished the third quarter with a total of 69 points. Then, early in the fourth quarter, Imhoff fouled out, leaving Buckner and 6′7″ Willie Naulls to contend with Wilt.

Just under eight minutes remained when Chamberlain broke his own record of 78. With the Warriors leading by a big margin, the team decided to keep feeding the ball to Wilt, to let him go for 100.

The Knicks did all they could to prevent it. In the last eight minutes, they held the ball for close to the full twenty-four seconds every time they had it. With five minutes left, Wilt had 89 points, and the Knicks started fouling the other Warrior players before they could feed Chamberlain. So the Warriors started immediately fouling the Knicks each time to get the ball back quicker.

Wilt went over two minutes without scoring, but then went on a binge and,

Wilt Chamberlain lived up to Frank McGuire's prediction.

with 1:19 left, he stuffed his 97th and 98th points. With forty-six seconds left, he took a pass and stuffed it again. Wilt was quickly mobbed by some two hundred fans, and players from both teams shook his hand.

Chamberlain had gone 36 for 63 from the field. The notoriously horrible free throw shooter hit a miraculous 28 of 32 (87.5%) from the line. He had scored 59 points in the second half, with 31 coming in the fourth quarter. Warriors guard Guy Rodgers had dished out 20 assists, but few noticed, for this night belonged entirely to Chamberlain, in a performance that probably will never be equaled.

In an ironic footnote to this historic event, the Knicks and Warriors played again the following night in New York. With time running out, Imhoff left the game and received a standing ovation from the Madison Square Garden crowd. Why? Because he had "held" Chamberlain to a mere 54 points!

The Blind Dribbler

When basketball was invented in 1891, the world of sports already had a history of playing for pay. Major-league baseball's National League was already in its sixteenth year when basketball came upon the scene. And it took the proponents of James Naismith's new sport only five years to join the ranks of the professionals.

Introduced at the YMCA in Springfield, Massachusetts, basketball spread quickly to other YMCAs around the United States and Canada. YMCA leaders soon became concerned that the rough new sport was taking up too much time in their gymnasiums, at the expense of their regular exercise programs.

Soon, YMCA basketball players around the country were being bounced from gyms and forced to find other buildings in which to pursue their new passion. They played in barns, warehouses, roller-skating rinks, and even on the slippery waxed floors of dance halls, where dancing was conducted before and after the games and sometimes at halftime.

The small groups of early basketball fans who would watch these games would help pay the rent for the buildings. Eventually, this led to the players being paid for the entertainment they were providing. According to *The NBA's Official Encyclopedia of Pro Basketball,* professional basketball began on a night in 1896 when the ballplayers in Trenton, New Jersey, rented the local Masonic Hall; they became the game's first pros for $15 each, with captain Fred Cooper earning an extra dollar.

The game's first pros were dressed flamboyantly. Wearing velvet trunks and long tights, they even sported frilled stockings that were designed by Cooper. (No wonder the former soccer player got paid an extra dollar: he doubled as captain and fashion coordinator.)

Among basketball followers, Cooper and teammate Al Bratton became known for developing a primitive but crowd-pleasing play in which they would pass the ball back and forth between them all the way from one end of the court to the other. And another Trenton player, Dutch Wohlfarth, amazed everyone by dribbling *without looking at the ball.* In fact, Wohlfarth earned the nickname the "blind dribbler," and was arguably basketball's first gate attraction.

What we take for granted as the simple art of dribbling without watching the ball was to fans in the 1890s as exciting as an "Air Jordan" slam dunk is to us today. And those fans were far more rowdy than today's spectators. As pro basketball spread, fans in certain areas became notorious for abusing opposing players and officials. Prospect Hall in Brooklyn earned the nickname the "Bucket of blood" when fans there tossed bottles at visiting players and jabbed them with lit cigarettes.

In fact, the invention of backboards was a direct result of the exuberance of these early spectators. Fans in the balcony became adept at knocking shots away from the basket, and some brought umbrellas to the games specifically for that purpose. While backboards eliminated that form of spectator participation, the fans continued to make their presence felt in a very physical manner.

All in all, those early years of basketball were rough—both on the court and off.

The Seven-Footer Who Said No to the Pros

Bob Kurland was born in St. Louis in 1924, and by the time he was thirteen years old, he had already grown to a height of 6′6″. Bob took up basketball when he entered high school, although he was not a natural athlete. Through hard work and continued growth, Kurland improved enough to play at Oklahoma A&M, which is now known as Oklahoma State.

As a sophomore, Kurland became a starter . . . and an All-American. He averaged 13 points per game, but made his mark by passing, setting devastating picks, and by standing under the basket blocking shots.

The NCAA became upset with this goaltending tactic perfected by Kurland and the great George Mikan at De Paul, and the next year they sent an official to watch Kurland in a game at Oklahoma University. The official sat on a platform above the goal to see if Kurland was illegally putting his hand over the top of the hoop. After the season, the NCAA outlawed blocking a shot on its downward arc, a tactic which to that point had been permissible.

Some skeptics predicted that the rule change would be fatal to Kurland's career. But that was hardly the case. Despite the new goaltending rule, Kurland had his best year in 1944–45, and the seven-foot junior led Oklahoma A&M to the national championship. Kurland averaged a whopping 17 points per game and scored 22 in the championship game against NYU.

In a special game to raise money for the Red Cross, Oklahoma A&M played De Paul, winners of the prestigious National Invitation Tournament. Oklahoma A&M won, 41–38, with Kurland outscoring Mikan, 14–9. Intimidated by

Kurland's ferocious shot blocking, De Paul hit on only 16 of their 96 shots from the field.

The next year, Oklahoma A&M won the national title again, the first time a college basketball team had ever won back-to-back titles. Kurland led the nation in scoring, averaging over 19 points per game.

Professional teams lined up with big money offers, one of which would have guaranteed him the staggering sum of $60,000 over five years. But Kurland turned them all down and went to work for Phillips Petroleum in Bartlesville, Oklahoma. Kurland had the makings of a good executive and Phillips had the best amateur basketball team in the country, the 66ers. They were about to get even better.

In 1948, the Phillips 66ers beat national champion University of Kentucky in the Olympic Trials. Then, in the Olympics at London, Kurland teamed with Alex Groza of Kentucky to lead the United States to an easy gold medal.

In the 1952 Olympics at Helsinki, Finland, Kurland combined with Clyde Lovellette of Kansas to again lead the USA to the finals, this time against the Soviet Union. Although the Russians used a stall, the Americans won the gold, 36–25.

Winning a second gold medal was enough for Bob. He returned to his desk in Oklahoma and gave up basketball, saying it was no longer fun. A potentially overpowering star in the pros, Bob Kurland never played a day of pro hoops. But he more than earned his place in the Basketball Hall of Fame.

Shotblocking specialist Bob Kurland

Death of a College Star

In March 1990, the basketball world was shaken by the sudden death of Hank Gathers, the Loyola-Marymount forward who had led the nation in scoring and rebounding the year before. Twenty-five years earlier, the life of another college scoring sensation had ended just as abruptly.

A three-sport high-school star in the copper-mining town of Anaconda, Montana, Wayne Estes was the quintessential All-American boy. He was All-State in football and basketball, and the state champion in the shot put and the discus. He was a fine student, too. But when he enrolled at Utah State in the fall of 1961, some thought he was too heavy and too clumsy to make it in college basketball.

At 6′6″ and weighing close to 250 pounds, Estes was nicknamed Baby Huey after the pot-bellied comic book character. But by the time the basketball season started, Wayne had dropped twenty-five pounds. He had also worked hard on his jump shot and on the running hook, which would become his trademark. Estes shot his way into national headlines, winning team MVP honors three years in a row and scoring over 33 points a game as a senior—second in the country to Rick Barry.

Bob Cousy called him "the greatest shooter in college basketball today." He was one of the game's finest ambassadors as well, never leaving the gym until he had signed autographs for every kid who wanted one, and answering at least five fan letters every day.

When Estes scored a career-high 48 points against Denver on February 8, 1965, he became Utah State's all-time leading scorer. But that was to be his final game.

After the game, Estes spent over an hour signing autographs, phoned his parents, then started walking back to campus with three friends. They came upon the scene of a car wreck, in which a car had crashed into a utility pole and knocked loose a high-tension wire. One of Wayne's friends walked under the wire, but the taller Estes brushed it with his forehead, then frantically grabbed the wire with both hands and was electrocuted.

Had Wayne been a few inches shorter, he would have cleared the 2,300-volt wire. Instead, his life came to an end at the age of twenty-one.

A public funeral was held for Estes at his high-school gym in Montana. Meanwhile, Utah State canceled their next game, with the gate receipts going into a Wayne Estes scholarship fund. Eight days after his death, a memorial service was held at the Utah State Fieldhouse. Over 5,000 people attended, and they saw Estes named to the Associated Press All-America Team, a month ahead of schedule, becoming the first posthumous All-American.

A large display case went up in the Fieldhouse, featuring Estes's jersey, warm-up suit, shoes, and awards. A year later, a federal district court jury awarded his family $100,000 in damages. Their suit had charged negligence on the part of the city of Logan, Utah, and the driver of the car that hit the utility pole. It was a small consolation for the loss of a life that had touched as many as Wayne Estes's did.

Bill Russell as USF's center

Bill Russell of the St. Louis Hawks?

Bill Russell is considered by many to be the man who revolutionized basketball in the '50s and '60s by emphasizing defense and by making the blocked shot an important part of the pro game. The 6′9″ center played in the NBA for thirteen years, all of them with the Boston Celtics. Eleven of those thirteen Celtics teams won championships. But Russell could easily have played for some team other than the Celtics after leading the University of San Francisco to back-to-back NCAA championships in 1955 and 1956. Because in the NBA draft in the spring of 1956, the Celtics had the number-six pick.

Before the draft, Russell announced that he would play for the US Olympic Team in Melbourne, Australia, in the fall before turning pro. That meant that whichever team drafted him would have to wait until early December to begin using his services. Also, Russell reportedly was seeking the rather pricey salary of $25,000 a year, with the option of signing with the Harlem Globetrotters for more than that. In fact, the Globetrotters made him a public offer of $50,000 a year to play for them.

The Rochester Royals had the first pick in the draft and decided they could not afford Russell's $25,000 price tag. They decided instead to draft Sihugo Green, a guard out of Duquesne. The St. Louis Hawks had the number-two pick, but they weren't interested in Russell either. Hawks owner Ben Kerner already had 6′9″ Bob Pettit as his drawing card, and the Hawks remained the only all-white team in the NBA. Kerner also objected to Russell's salary demand. The Minneapolis Lakers owned the number-three pick and they intended to use it properly—by drafting Bill Russell.

Coach Red Auerbach of the Celtics, realizing that only a trade could bring Russell to Boston, phoned Kerner in St. Louis and offered him veteran center Easy Ed Macauley in exchange for the number-two pick in the draft. Macauley was already twenty-eight years old, but he was an NBA All-Star who had been born in St. Louis. And Macauley had been an All-American in college at St. Louis University.

Needless to say, Macauley's name caught Kerner's attention, but the Hawks owner insisted that the Celtics also give them 6′4″ forward Cliff Hagan, whom Boston had drafted two years earlier. Hagan had just completed two years in the military and was about to enter the NBA. Wisely, Auerbach agreed to include Hagan in the deal, and a dynasty was born in Boston.

The Celtics waited until December 22 for Russell to join them, but he was well worth waiting for. Led by Bob Cousy, Bill Sharman, Russell, and another rookie, Tommy Heinsohn, the Celtics marched to the NBA finals that year against who else—the St. Louis Hawks. In the deciding seventh game, the Celtics won the championship in double overtime, 125–123, as Russell scored 19 points and pulled down 32 rebounds. And to think he could have been playing for the Hawks.

The Fort Wayne Freeze

On November 22, 1950, the defending NBA champion Minneapolis Lakers were hosting the Fort Wayne Pistons at the Minneapolis Auditorium, where the Lakers had won 29 straight in a streak dating back to the previous season. The Lakers were led by dominant center George Mikan, the league's leading scorer for the second year in a row.

In an effort to contain the Lakers, specifically Mikan, who averaged 28 points a game that year, the Pistons decided to hang on to the ball. The 24-second clock was not yet in use, and the Lakers refused to come outside to try to get the ball. At the end of a less-than-scintillating first quarter, the Pistons led 8–7.

The referees could do nothing to speed up the game, and the fans were irate when the first half ended—even though their Lakers held a 13–11 lead. The Piston players had to surround their coach, Murray Mendenhall, to keep outraged spectators away from him on the way to the locker room.

Once they were safely inside, Mendenhall asked his players if they wanted to continue the stall, and their decision was a unanimous "yes."

So, Fort Wayne's freeze continued after halftime, and at the end of three quarters, the Lakers led the Pistons by one point 17–16. With four minutes left in the game, the Lakers still led by one point, 18–17, but the Pistons had the ball. At that point, the Pistons decided to play for the last shot.

Soon after play resumed, a Fort Wayne pass sailed out of bounds, but the officials ruled that the Lakers had deflected it. The Minneapolis fans went wild, and play was stopped for several minutes while the court was cleared of refuse that had been hurled at the referees.

The Pistons inbounded the ball again and held it until ten seconds remained, when Piston center Larry Foust cut across the top of the key, took a pass, and drove toward the hoop. Foust flung up a short, running hook shot that went off Mikan's fingertips and in and gave the Pistons a 19–18 lead. The Lakers only had time for a desperation half-court shot, which missed at the buzzer. The Pistons had won.

Thirty-seven points by two teams remains the lowest total in NBA history, as each team sank only 4 field goals. Mikan scored 15 points in the losing cause, but his teammates (including a young Bud Grant, later the great coach of pro football's Minnesota Vikings) managed only 3.

While the Minneapolis fans were infuriated, Fort Wayne fans turned out one thousand strong at the train station at eight a.m. the following day to welcome

LOWEST SCORING GAME IN NBA HISTORY

November 22, 1950 at Minneapolis

FORT WAYNE (19)

Player	Pos.	FGA	FGM	FTA	FTM	Reb.	Ast.	PF	Pts.
Fred Schaus	F	1	0	3	3	0	1	0	3
Jack Kerris	F	1	0	4	2	2	0	5	2
Larry Foust	C	2	1	1	1	1	0	3	3
Bob Harris		0	0	1	0	1	0	1	0
John Hargis	G	1	1	0	0	0	1	0	2
Ralph Johnson		1	0	0	0	0	1	1	0
John Oldham	G	5	1	4	3	4	0	2	5
Paul Armstrong		2	1	2	2	0	0	1	4
Total		13	4	15	11	8	3	13	19

MINNEAPOLIS LAKERS (18)

Player	Pos.	FGA	FGM	FTA	FTM	Reb.	Ast.	PF	Pts.
Jim Pollard	F	1	0	1	1	1	1	2	1
Bud Grant		0	0	0	0	0	1	1	0
Vern Mikkelsen	F	2	0	0	0	3	0	2	0
Joe Hutton		0	0	0	0	0	0	0	0
George Mikan	C	11	4	11	7	4	0	1	15
Slater Martin	G	2	0	3	0	1	2	2	0
Bob Harrison	G	2	0	2	2	0	0	3	2
Arnie Ferrin		0	0	0	0	0	0	0	0
Total		18	4	17	10	9	4	11	18

Score by Periods:	1st	2nd	3rd	4th	Totals
Fort Wayne Pistons	8	3	5	3	19
Minneapolis Lakers	7	6	4	1	18

Referees—Jocko Collins and Stan Stutz. Attendance—7,021.

back their team. Ironically, the Pistons beat the Lakers again in Fort Wayne the next night, 73–63, without using the stall. But the Lakers went on to win the Western Division title.

NBA commissioner Maurice Podoloff thought the 19–18 game had shown a strong disregard for the fans, and instructed the league's owners and coaches to never let it happen again. You can be sure that 37 points will remain the lowest two-team total in NBA history.

The Father of Basketball

Unlike baseball, whose inventor is subject to debate, basketball indisputably was the brainchild of one man, Dr. James Naismith, who invented the game back in 1891. Some people surmised that Naismith received his inspiration from the ancient Mayan Indian game of *pok-ta-pok,* which featured a stone ring set in a side wall, through which the players would propel a small ball. But Naismith denied receiving any inspiration from the Central American game.

Few people today know that the inventor of this great American sport was a Canadian. Naismith was born in the small country town of Almonte, Ontario, in 1861. He graduated from McGill University in Montreal, then studied three years at the Presbyterian Theological Seminary with the intention of becoming a minister. But Naismith loved athletics. He had played football and lacrosse in college, and decided that he could help his fellow man in ways other than preaching.

Naismith decided to enter the International YMCA Training School in Spring-

Dr. James Naismith started it all.

field, Massachusetts, which is now known as Springfield College. It was there that the demand for a new game became pressing. James Naismith answered that need.

In the fall of 1891, Naismith and his colleagues in Springfield realized that the members of their gymnasium classes were losing interest. Dr. Luther Gulick, the head of the physical education department, was looking for a new game to increase enthusiasm. If necessity is the mother of invention, then in this case, James Naismith became the father.

Naismith's idea may have come from the childhood game, Duck On A Rock, in which kids would try to knock a grapefruit-sized rock off the top of a big boulder by tossing smaller rocks at it. While at McGill, Naismith had helped keep rugby players occupied during the off-season by having them flip balls into an empty box set on the floor of the gym.

Naismith's gym class at Springfield had eighteen students, so he devised a game for two teams of nine players within the small gym. Once he had decided to use a soccer ball, Naismith's critical decision (his brainstorm, in fact) was to place the goals ten feet above the ground.

Finding the proper goals was another matter. Naismith was looking for two boxes about 18″ square, but then the school janitor, "Pop" Stebbins, came up with a couple of old peach baskets. He nailed them to the wooden track that hung above the gym and the first game soon began.

A few years after inventing basketball, Naismith left Springfield. He earned a degree in medicine but did not practice. Instead, he joined the faculty at the University of Kansas, as director of chapel and professor of physical education. And, yes, he was also the Jayhawks' basketball coach for ten years. Naismith felt strongly that basketball was primarily for fun and exercise, not competition, and his Kansas teams had losing records.

Naismith taught classes at Kansas for almost forty years, during which his "invention" grew to become an international favorite. When he died at the age of seventy-eight in 1939, he was probably unaware of just how large a contribution he had made to the world of sports, as it would be several decades before basketball became the universal phenomenon it is today.

The First Basketball Game

Back in 1891, when James Naismith invented his new game at the International YMCA Training School in Springfield, Massachusetts, he had eighteen students in his gymnasium class. So the first basketball game had nine players on a team. Had his class been larger, there would have been more men per side, because Naismith envisioned games being played by teams of up to forty players each. After all, the game had been invented as a way to erase the boredom of exercise, and Naismith wanted as many people involved as possible.

The first basketball game was played in a small gym only 50 feet by 35 feet, with half-bushel baskets 15 inches wide nailed to the wooden running track hanging above the gym. The ball used was a soccer ball, and yes, they did have to retrieve the ball from the bottom of the basket after a goal was made. This didn't prove to be much of a problem on that first day, though, as only one goal was made in the sport's initial game.

That's right: After two fifteen-minute halves, the score, under Naismith's original rules, was 1–0. But that one basket was somewhat spectacular, a twenty-five-foot heave from midcourt by a student named William R. Chase.

Naismith's original rules included many of the features of today's game. Neither running with the ball nor striking an opponent was allowed. But free throws were not invented for another three years. Originally, when a player committed his second foul, he had to sit out, with his team shorthanded, until the next basket was scored.

The eighteen physical education students who played in that first game in 1891 are all enshrined in the Basketball Hall of Fame in Springfield, not far from where the game was played. In honor of their teacher, the students first wanted to call the game Naismith ball, but Naismith refused to allow it. Instead, he accepted the name submitted by Frank Mahan, one of his students, and it has been basketball ever since.

During their Christmas vacation that year, the students returned to their homes, where many of them introduced basketball to their local YMCAs. Five of the eighteen were from Canada and one was from Japan. In the years to come, one of the players went to China, and another to India. Less than a year after that first game, basketball was played throughout the United States; within a few years, it was a worldwide game. The sport had spread like wildfire, partially because those original eighteen players and their fellow students had become missionaries of basketball.

The Professional Debut of Lew Alcindor

Still known as Lew Alcindor when he entered the NBA, the man we now know as Kareem Abdul-Jabbar had been closely chronicled since his high-school days at Power Memorial in New York City. Already a national celebrity when he entered UCLA in 1965, the 7′1½″ center enhanced his reputation by leading the Bruins to three straight national championships, averaging 26 points and 16 rebounds a game.

Alcindor's NBA rights belonged to the Milwaukee Bucks, who had won the crucial coin flip from the league's other last-place club, the Phoenix Suns. But the Bucks also had to contend with a big offer to Alcindor from the ABA New York Nets. Eventually, Milwaukee signed him to a five-year contract for a reported $1.4 million. (That's a bench player's salary in today's NBA.)

Alcindor immediately replaced the veteran Wayne Embry as Milwaukee's starting center. Coached by Larry Costello, the Bucks had Jon McGlocklin and Flynn Robinson at guard and Greg Smith and rookie Bob Dandrige at forward. In their first game of 1969, the Bucks would oppose the Detroit Pistons, with their

6′11″ center and longtime standout Walt Bellamy.

Alcindor's first pro game was on a Saturday afternoon, October 18, 1969, at the Milwaukee Arena. The game was nationally televised by ABC as a *Wide World of Sports Special,* almost three months before their regular NBA Game of the Week would begin, because the sports world had been waiting for this one.

The opening tip was won by Alcindor, and eighteen seconds later, Lew hit his first pro shot, a twelve-foot turnaround. Alcindor scored 14 points in the first quarter and 5 in the second as the Bucks took a 60–53 halftime lead. When interviewed at halftime on ABC, Alcindor said that despite scoring 19 points, he was disappointed in his shooting.

In the second half, the Bucks maintained their lead and won the game 119–110. When it was over, Alcindor had scored 29 points, hitting 12 out of 29 shots

Lew Alcindor

from the floor. He had pulled down 12 rebounds, handed out 6 assists, and blocked 3 shots. And he had played the entire forty-eight minutes.

It was a heroic debut in most people's minds, but Alcindor was not impressed. In a postgame interview, he berated himself, saying, "I didn't care too much for my play. I made a lot of mistakes." Perhaps those critical remarks were an indication of just how special a star this man was going to be—and the high standards he would measure himself against over twenty-one incredible seasons.

The Worst Team in NBA History

The 1971–72 Philadelphia 76ers were a bad team, winning 30 and losing 52, to finish 26 games behind division champion Boston. But four other teams were worse, including the Portland Trail Blazers, who went 18–64. Following the season, however, the Sixers were dealt a crushing blow when a judge in Richmond, Virginia, ruled that the team's top scorer, Billy Cunningham, would have to play the next season for the Carolina Cougars of the ABA. Cunningham had previously signed with Carolina, but claimed the Cougars had broken the contract by missing a bonus payment.

The Sixers had already lost their coach, as Jack Ramsay resigned after the season, claiming the team was uncoachable. Several potential coaches turned down the job before young Roy Rubin was lured away from Long Island University and given a three-year contract. Just hours after taking the job, Rubin learned that he would not have Cunningham on his team. That was a sign of things to come.

A series of bad trades and ill-advised draft choices had left the 76ers with a team that was low on size and experience, and stocked with rejects from other teams. They still had former backcourt star Hal Greer, but he was thirty-six years old and rode the bench. Rookie Fred Boyd started at guard along with Fred Carter, and Boyd received an instant education from the likes of Oscar Robertson, Jerry West, and Walt Frazier. Carter turned out to be an outstanding scorer, averaging 20 points, but the team had no playmaker. And the frontcourt was a mess. Leroy Ellis was acquired to plug the middle, but couldn't do the job. Neither could anyone else on the forward line.

Before the season began, one of Rubin's friends joked, "Roy, you're going to lose 82 games in a row." For a while, it seemed he might be right, as the Sixers lost their first 15 games before mixing in a victory. On January 24, with their record at 4–47, General Manager Don Desjardins fired Rubin, despite his three-year contract, and replaced him with one of his players, veteran guard Kevin Loughery.

Rubin had lasted 105 days on the job, during which he lost 47 games and forty-five pounds. Loughery, who was thirty-two years old and had recently injured his knee, was given a three-year contract as player-coach. Ironically, Loughery had asked to be traded in November when he became fed up with the team's losing ways. Now it was his team to run, and things didn't get any better.

Under Loughery, the Sixers went 3–26, to finish with a record of 9–73. Their winning percentage of .110 remains the lowest in NBA history. They used a total of nineteen players, including Boyd and Manny Leaks, who had the misfortune of appearing in all 82 games. And in the midst of it all came the longest losing streak in NBA history.

Beginning January 9, 1973, the Sixers had lost 9 in a row when Loughery replaced Rubin as coach. But the losing continued. On February 10, the Sixers lost to Portland 126–121, to set a new NBA record with their 19th consecutive defeat. The next night, they lost to the Lakers 108–90, for their 20th loss in a row.

Their next game was against the Milwaukee Bucks, who would go 60–22 that year. The Sixers hung in there, and the game was tied at 104–all in the closing seconds when Fred Boyd took a jump shot that was blocked by Milwaukee's Dick Cunningham. The referee called goaltending, the Sixers had the winning basket, and the streak had ended.

Twenty consecutive losses in one season remains the NBA record. (Two other teams did lose 19 in a row: the Los Angeles Clippers from December 30, 1988, to February 6, 1989, and the 1981–82 Cleveland Cavaliers, who lost their final 19 games.) What was it like to be a part of that nightmare? Carter, who led the team in scoring, recalled, "It was embarrassing. You snuck in and out of town hoping nobody would notice you. You never said you were a 76er."

The club ended the season with another losing string of 13 games, prompting Loughery to bail out on his three-year contract. He left to coach the New York Nets of the ABA, while Gene Shue was brought in to pick up the pieces in Philadelphia. To Shue's credit, the team won 25 games the next season—hardly a record to brag about, but a major improvement for the worst team in NBA history.

Cazzie vs. Bradley

The 1964 Eastern Collegiate Athletic Conference Holiday Festival at Madison Square Garden featured two of college basketball's headline players, Cazzie Russell of Michigan and Bill Bradley of Princeton. The two All-Americans appeared destined to meet head-on in the tournament's second round, and that's exactly what happened.

Russell led his Michigan Wolverines into the second round with a 36-point outing against Manhattan, as Michigan won 90–77. Bradley duplicated Russell's feat by scoring 36 against Syracuse in a 79–69 Princeton win. Somewhat overlooked in a losing effort were the 28 points pumped in by another future NBA great, Syracuse guard Dave Bing. But it was the Russell-Bradley matchup that everyone was anxiously awaiting.

Both stars were 6′5″, although Russell was listed as a guard and Bradley as a forward. Another difference was that Russell was only a junior while Bradley was a senior. Their teams' strategies differed greatly, however; Michigan played a fast-paced running game, while Princeton hoped to contain the Wolverine fast

Michigan All-American Cazzie Russell

break and waited patiently for high-percentage shots.

On December 30, 1964, the Michigan-Princeton game drew a capacity crowd of over 18,000 to the old Garden. They got their money's worth. In the first half, Bradley went wild with 23 points, while Cazzie was held to only 8 by Princeton guard Don Rodenback. But Princeton carried a lead of only 39–37 into the locker room.

Michigan put on a full-court press in the second half that forced Bradley to help bring the ball upcourt. He responded brilliantly, and Princeton opened up a 13-point lead with about four minutes to play. Unfortunately, that's when Bradley fouled out of the game. He left with 41 points, to a rousing standing ovation—the last occasion Tiger fans would have to cheer.

With Bradley gone, Michigan scored 10 straight points, 6 of them by Russell, and moments later, Cazzie completed a three-point play to tie it 78–78. Princeton then missed a shot, and Michigan decided to play for the last shot. With three seconds remaining, Cazzie went up with a jumper and hit it, to win the game 80–78.

Bradley had won the hearts of the crowd, but Russell had won the game. A few years later, the New York fans had them both, as the two stars became teammates on the great New York Knicks team, which went on to win the NBA championship in 1970. That team included other perennial All-Stars Walt Frazier, Dave DeBusschere, and Willis Reed.

The Start of Big-time Basketball

In the early 1930s, there were ten colleges in the New York City area that played top-notch college basketball. Student interest was high, but none of the schools had a gym large enough to seat all the students who wanted to see the games. NYU, for example, had a student body of 7,500 and a 1,500-seat gym. Similar conditions existed at Fordham, City College, and several of the other schools. Many of the students and the general public were being shut out of college basketball.

In 1931, with the Depression hurting everyone, New York mayor Jimmy Walker asked the city's sportswriters to promote some benefit basketball games for the Unemployment Relief Fund. The resulting triple-header packed Madison Square Garden, and an all-day seven-game program in 1933 attracted 20,000 fans.

One of the writers who helped promote those games was Ned Irish, whose salary at the *New York World Telegram* had been reduced from $60 a week to $48. Irish saw the future of basketball as a spectator sport and came up with a plan to capitalize on it. He proposed renting Madison Square Garden for doubleheaders matching the New York schools against teams from other parts of the country. Irish would guarantee the Garden $4,000 as a rental fee, plus a share of any revenues above that, and he would handle all the details. With their arena unbooked several nights a week, the Garden officials readily agreed.

On December 29, 1934, the first doubleheader at the Garden drew a sell-out crowd to see St. John's against Westminster and NYU against Notre Dame. Irish made more money that night than he could in six months as a sportswriter. He instantly became a full-time promoter, and his first eight doubleheaders averaged over 12,000 fans a night.

Soon Irish was promoting games in Philadelphia, where the local teams included Temple, St. Joseph's, and Pennsylvania. Then, in Buffalo, he staged doubleheaders featuring St. Bonaventure, Canisius, and Niagara.

Irish went on to become the president of Madison Square Garden and the founder of the New York Knicks. But he will be best remembered as the man who introduced the intersectional college doubleheader, a move that, more than any other, made basketball a big-time sport.

Mr. Basketball of the First Half-Century

In the 1940s and '50s, George Mikan was as dominant as any player who has ever played the game. A 6′10″ center, Mikan revolutionized basketball as the first great big man. As a scorer, shotblocker, and rebounder, Mikan led his team to seven pro championships in an eight-year period. And, as a gate attraction, Mikan and his Minneapolis Lakers were most responsible for making the NBA a financial success.

Wearing thick glasses and the familiar number 99 on his jersey, Mikan was the leading vote-getter for the all-league team seven years in a row—the equivalent of today's MVP award. This seven-year reign as pro basketball's most outstanding player is unequaled in the history of the game. His record as a winner also speaks for itself. His teams played a total of 22 playoff series and won 21 of them.

Mikan's game was played under the basket, where he would use his height and his 245 pounds of bulk to great advantage. In the first two years of the NBA he was virtually unstoppable, leading the league in scoring with averages of 27 and 28 points a game, while only two other players averaged over 20 points a game. When every possible defense against him had failed, the league itself finally changed the rules to help contain him.

In attempting to neutralize Mikan, teams tried fouling him, but the tactic rarely worked because George was a fine free throw shooter. But he had to endure all sorts of physical abuse, including a total of five broken bones and four broken fingers during his career, plus a grand total of 166 stitches. To stop him, the NBA in 1952 widened the foul lane from six to twelve feet, but the rule had little impact on Mikan. His scoring average dropped only slightly, to 24 points a game.

Centered around Mikan, the Laker offense was a patient one, as they waited for big George to get open underneath for one of his short-running hook shots. It often took thirty seconds or more for them to get off a shot. When the NBA adopted the 24-second clock in 1954, some said it was another move designed to shut down the Lakers.

This time the tactic worked. Mikan, who had just turned thirty, retired as an active player before the next season began. And the Lakers' string of championships came to an end.

Mikan went on to become the Lakers' general manager, earned his law degree, and later became the first commissioner of the upstart American Basketball Association in 1967. But those achievements pale compared with the impact Mikan had on the game as an active player. In recognition of his accomplishments, Mikan was voted the greatest player in the first fifty years of basketball in an Associated Press poll.

George Mikan, with DePaul coach Ray Meyer

George Mikan's Path to Stardom

Born in Joliet, Illinois, in 1924, George Mikan grew up in an Old World family with its roots in Yugoslavia. His parents emphasized the importance of a well-rounded education, and young George took eight years of piano lessons at school. Eventually, he received a degree in piano from a conservatory, and his keyboard experience turned out to be invaluable to George on the basketball court as well. Because his fingers developed such strength and dexterity, he could control the ball on his fingertips much more easily than most other players.

Although he was already 6′4″ at the age of thirteen, Mikan didn't play much basketball in high school. He had to quit one high-school team when they wouldn't let him play in glasses. He also suffered a broken leg that sidelined him for a long period of time.

Mikan enrolled on his own at De Paul University in Chicago, where a new young coach named Ray Meyer turned George into a star. Mikan was then a 6′8″ forward without a lot of coordination. Recalled Meyer, "We just wanted him to go into a corner and get lost." Instead, Meyer worked with Mikan for hours on end, devising special drills to overcome his awkwardness. Meyer had him work out every day, skipping rope, shadowboxing, punching a bag, and sparring to develop coordination. He even hired a woman to give Mikan dancing lessons.

On the basketball court Mikan worked on his ballhandling with smaller, quicker players. And he worked slavishly on the hook shot, which eventually made him unstoppable. He would take 200 right-hand hooks and 200 left-hand hooks every day of the year.

After a rough freshman year in which his main value was in blocking shots, Mikan became an All-American in each of his last three years. He led the nation in scoring in 1945 and 1946, and led De Paul to the NIT championship in 1945 by averaging 40 points a game in the tournament, including 53 in one game—a Madison Square Garden record.

When Mikan left De Paul, he was a polished 6′10″ center, and he signed a five-year contract with the Chicago Gears of the National Basketball League, a deal worth $60,000. He quickly became the big gate attraction who led the Minneapolis Lakers to a string of NBA titles, and led the NBA to financial success.

Through it all, Mikan never forgot to credit Ray Meyer. In George's own words, "Ray was a slave driver. But he was just what I needed. He taught me everything I know."

The Record That Got No Respect

Just about any basketball fan can tell you that Wilt Chamberlain holds the NBA record for points in one game—100. Many know that the single-game rebound record also belongs to Wilt the Stilt, who had 55 one night. But how many are aware of the record holder for assists in one game? Magic Johnson? Isiah Thomas? Bob Cousy? Oscar Robertson?

All those noted playmakers take a back seat to Kevin Porter, the 5′11″ guard who played eleven years in the league in the '70s and early '80s. Porter piled up 29 assists in a game in 1978 to set a record that is one of the least recognized in the NBA record book. To be truthful, it is also one of the least respected.

At the time Porter set the record, he was playing for the New Jersey Nets. He had recently been traded from Detroit, where he hadn't gotten along with Pistons coach Herb Brown. The Nets were Porter's third team in five years, and despite leading the league in assists, Porter was a frequent target of criticism around the league. His detractors claimed that Kevin hogged the ball, leading to his many assists, but also to numerous turnovers. In fact, Porter *was* leading the league in turnovers as well as assists.

On February 24, the Nets were on their home court in Piscataway, New Jersey, facing the Houston Rockets. The Nets opened up a comfortable lead, led by Porter's playmaking and the shooting of John Williamson, who scored 39 points, and Bernard King, who added 35. But the focus turned to Porter late in the fourth quarter when Nets coach Kevin Loughery was informed that Porter had a shot at the one-game assist record of 28. Bob Cousy had set the record in 1959, and Guy

Kevin Porter

Rodgers had tied it in 1963.

In the closing minutes, the Nets made sure that any shot they took would carry with it a Porter assist. In the last minute of play, Howard Porter (no relation) scored off a feed from Kevin Porter to break the record. The Nets won 126–112, and Loughery emphasized the team's performance in his postgame remarks, saying, "It was just a great team game for us. Porter is a great passer and he played a great game, but he needed the shooters to chalk up the assists."

Porter also declined to emphasize the new record. "I've been committing too many turnovers and needless fouls lately," he said. "So I was really glad to have a big game. But this is pro basketball and the name of the game is winning, not records."

And what did Cousy think about having his name erased from the record book? He may actually have been relieved. When asked his reaction, Cousy replied frankly, "That record wasn't legitimate. I got it the day we scored 173 points or something in a game where everyone on the team seemed bent on scoring a career high." And a look at the record book reveals that the Celtics did score 173 points that night against the Lakers, an NBA record for a non-overtime game.

While Cousy may not have cared about losing the record, many believe that in reality he still owns it. In Cousy's day, for the passer to get an assist, a shot had to come immediately without any moves or fakes by the shooter. And assists were rarely given unless a pass led to a layup. The feeling was that for an assist to be awarded, the pass had to be more instrumental in creating the basket than the shot.

Since basketball scorekeeping has changed significantly over the years, making assists much easier to come by, the 28 assists by Cousy and Rodgers may have been much tougher to achieve than Porter's 29. And that may be the biggest reason that Porter's mark remains one of the NBA's least respected records.

The Duel of the Century

Promoted as the Duel of the Century, the Harlem Globetrotters took on pro basketball's best team in February 1948 when they met George Mikan and the Minneapolis Lakers at Chicago Stadium. Led by center Goose Tatum, the Globetrotters had won 101 games in a row, but the Lakers didn't take the streak very seriously. The Lakers were on their way to winning the championship of the National Basketball League, with Mikan the unanimous Most Valuable Player.

The game received a tremendous buildup in the press, and a crowd of 17,853 packed the Stadium to see it. Mikan later admitted that all the hype caused him to try to outdo Tatum and personally win the game for his team. And while he outscored the Goose, 24–9, he was victimized by a couple of the Globetrotter's ball-handling tricks. On one occasion, Mikan dropped his arms while watching Tatum's antics, allowing Goose to fire a pass to an unguarded teammate under the basket. And Globetrotter veteran Duke Cumberland even placed the ball on Mikan's head and got away with it.

But this game was not for laughs, and it came down to the final minute, when Mikan hit a free throw to tie it 59–59. Ermer Robinson of the Globetrotters then controlled the ball until the final seconds, when he sank a long shot to win the game 61–59.

The teams played a rematch at the Stadium in 1949, and this time over 20,000 turned out. They watched the Globetrotters control the game from start to finish, winning 49–45. But Laker fans claimed their team would have won if two of their starters, Jim Pollard and Don Carlson, had not missed the game with injuries. Although it sounded like an alibi, Laker supporters may very well have been right.

A few weeks later, the Lakers crushed the Globetrotters 68–53 before a sellout crowd in Minneapolis. During the next two years, the teams played three more games, all in front of capacity crowds. The Lakers won all three, giving them four straight wins over the Trotters, by an average margin of 13 points.

The last game of the series was played in February 1951. Globetrotters owner Abe Saperstein had just made a movie about his team and badly wanted a victory to help attract viewers. But he was frustrated again, as Mikan scored 47 points in a 72–68 Laker win. The next day, Saperstein called Lakers owner Max Winter and canceled the next scheduled game, apparently conceding that his team could not win.

The Globetrotters then played an annual series against a team of college all-stars, winning 146 and losing 66 over a span of twelve years. But their claim of being as good as the best professional teams was effectively ended by George Mikan and the Minneapolis Lakers.

The First Great "Sixth Man"

In today's NBA, every team has a talented "sixth man" who comes off the bench during each game to give the team a lift. Sometimes he's a scorer, sometimes a playmaker, and sometimes a rebounder. The league even honors these specialists with their own award, the Sixth Man Award, which was won first by the 76ers' Bobby Jones in 1982–83. But until Frank Ramsey came along, there was no such role player on an NBA team.

Ramsey was only 6′3″, but he had been a pivotman at the University of Kentucky, where he and Cliff Hagan led the Wildcats to an undefeated season in 1953–54. Both Ramsey and Hagan were drafted into the military after that season, but Celtic general manager Red Auerbach had the foresight to draft them and wait.

Hagan was subsequently traded to St. Louis in the Bill Russell deal, while Ramsey joined the Celtics in 1954. His versatility was an immediate asset to the Celtics, as he averaged 11 points a game coming off the bench in his rookie year. About two-thirds of his playing time came at forward and one-third in the backcourt.

Ramsey loved being the man who could ignite the Boston offense. He was a streaky shooter and was very adept at drawing fouls. Although he usually played less than half the game, Frank increased his scoring average to 16 points a game in his third season. And he was usually on the court if the game was close at the end, as he was superb in the clutch.

At forward, Ramsey often had to guard much bigger men, like 6′8″ Bailey Howell and Rudy LaRusso. But Frank often ran rings around them. And he never complained about being a substitute, saying, "I'd rather be a sub on a great team than a regular on a losing one."

When Ramsey began to slow down, he taught his craft to the man who would succeed him and eventually surpass his performance. Thirty-one years old when John Havlicek joined the Celtics in 1962, Frank readily accepted the job of training his replacement as the team's sixth man. Ramsey spent hours and hours working with Havlicek, who was a notoriously poor shooter at the time. But Havlicek had the same ability to outrun his opponent, and at 6′5″, was bigger and stronger than Ramsey.

Ramsey taught Havlicek the art of drawing fouls and how to break past his

Frank Ramsey

man on a fast break. And he also taught him to sit on the bench with his jacket draped loosely on his shoulders, so he could quickly get into the game without unzipping his jacket and pants. That's right: Frank Ramsey even set the standard for how a sixth man should dress.

Eighty Men on the Court?

When James Naismith invented basketball in 1891, he believed the game could be played by teams of up to forty players on a side, with the ideal number being nine. He even outlined the positions for a nine-man team—a goalkeeper and two guards (who would prevent the opposition from scoring), three center men (who would be the playmakers), and three forwards (two wings and a "home man," who would do most of the scoring). Within two years, teams were limited in size to either nine-men or five-men, and in 1897 the five-man team became mandatory.

The idea of a free throw after fouls was not instituted until 1894, three years after the game was invented. When first introduced, free throws were shot from twenty feet and counted one point, the same as a field basket. One year later, they moved the foul line in to the present fifteen-foot distance, and in 1896, they began counting field goals as 2 points.

Before 1924, the captain chose one player to be sort of a designated shooter, shooting all of his team's free throws. In 1924, the rule was changed to force the player who had been fouled to take the free throw.

Naismith's original rules called for two fifteen-minute halves, with a five-minute intermission. Just two years later, halves were extended to twenty minutes each, with an eleven-minute halftime break. The original rules allowed for sudden death to break ties. It was not until 1907 that a five-minute overtime period was adopted.

The equipment used to play the game changed rather rapidly, too. The first games were played with soccer balls. As early as 1893, however, balls made specifically for basketball came on the market, balls just about the same size as the one we use today.

The original peach baskets were phased out quickly. They were replaced by wire baskets that made it possible to remove the ball from the basket with a long stick, rather than having to use a step ladder. In 1894, the baskets were enlarged at the top from the original fifteen inches to the current eighteen-inch diameter. And finally, in 1906, open-bottomed nets came into use.

The uniforms evolved rapidly, too. Naismith's original teams wore long pants and long-sleeved jerseys. Some early players wore football or baseball pants, or gym tights covered with velvet trunks. Soon, short-sleeved and sleeveless shirts became the standard jersey.

Dr. Naismith's original idea laid a solid foundation on which to build. It didn't take long for him and his colleagues to make critical changes that improved the game and made it more like the sport we love today.

The Buffalo Germans, The First Great Team

Basketball's first great team, the Buffalo Germans, were organized in 1895, just four years after the sport was invented. Their founder, Frederick Burkhardt, was the physical director of a YMCA on the east side of Buffalo, the home of many families of German extraction. At the time of the team's formation, the players were just fourteen years old. None of them imagined that the team would last until the 1920s.

The Germans became famous in 1901 when they won the Pan-American Exposition; the basketball games were played in Buffalo on a grass court, with the players wearing cleats to keep from slipping. In one game that year, they de-

Buffalo Germans player-manager Al Heerdt

feated Hobart College 134–0. This was during a time when scores were generally in the twenties and thirties.

In 1904, the Germans won an "exhibition" tournament held at the Olympic Games in St. Louis, and were thought of as the best team in the world. Although no national tournaments were held between 1904 and 1910, the Germans cemented their reputation by touring as a professional team.

Led by their stars, Al Heerdt and Eddie Miller, the Germans once reeled off a streak of 111 consecutive victories before finally losing to a team in Herkimer, New York, in 1910. By the time their streak ended, the Germans were traveling as far as Kansas and receiving up to $500 for a three-game series. On one of their trips they defeated the Carlisle Indians, who were led by Jim Thorpe.

Frank Basloe, owner of the Herkimer team that had snapped the winning streak, founded a team in Oswego, New York, called the Indians, that was designed to challenge the Germans. During the 1913–14 season, the Indians defeated the Germans three times in a very rough four-game series. To beat the Germans, Basloe imported ball-handling sensation Oscar "Swede" Grimstead all the way from New York City. The Indians went on to win 121 games and lost only 6 the following year, but the Germans continued their winning ways as well.

When the Germans finally disbanded in 1929, their record was 792–86, a winning percentage of .902. By then the original players had retired, but one of the early stars, Al Heerdt, was managing the team.

Two years later, in 1931, the original Buffalo Germans reassembled for an exhibition game, a reunion of sorts. The team of fifty-one-year-olds went out on the court against a popular local team and won by a single point.

Buffalo may not have lasted as an NBA city, but it was home to basketball's first great team, the Buffalo Germans.

The World's Tallest Basketball Player

Standing 7′3″ and weighing 235 pounds, Wade "Swede" Halbrook entered the NBA in 1960, billed as The World's Tallest Basketball Player. At the time, he was the tallest player ever in the league, but his nickname Swede was actually a misnomer, as his ancestry was German and Dutch.

Halbrook was one of the NBA's most unusual characters. A nonconformist who was shy and introverted, his hobby was knitting, a diversion that helped him relax. When he joined the Syracuse Nationals in 1960, he carried yarn and needles with him on the road, but he eventually stopped using them in public because of all the kidding. He still knitted in the privacy of his hotel room, though, and at one particularly boring banquet, Swede amused himself by taking out his needles and knitting a few stitches.

Halbrook was a private person who was polite but uncooperative with reporters who tried to get him to open up. He was a casual dresser who preferred sport shirts to suits, and sources say he suffered emotionally as a youth when his family could not afford to dress him in good-looking, well-fitting clothes.

Swede spent just two seasons in the NBA as Syracuse's backup center. Playing twelve to fifteen minutes a game, Halbrook averaged 5.5 points and 7 rebounds while holding his own defensively against the likes of Bill Russell and Wilt Chamberlain. Some Syracuse fans cheered him as "The People's Choice," but others booed him for not taking better advantage of his height.

There were those who accused him of being lazy. On more than one occasion, Syracuse coach Alex Hannum threatened to release Halbrook in order to get him to play harder. And ultimately, even when giving his all, Halbrook was too slow for the league. But that was hardly the case when Swede first burst upon the national scene.

The child of parents who stood only 6′1″ and 5′9″, Halbrook shot up to a height of seven feet at the age of sixteen in Portland, Oregon. The high-school basketball coach persuaded him to come out for basketball, and Halbrook led his team to the state title as a senior in 1952. He scored 71 points in one game, and received seventy-five college scholarship offers, the most ever by a basketball player from the Northwest.

Halbrook chose to stay close to home and attended Oregon State, where the fraternity that landed him custom-built an eight-foot bed for him. The team traveled in a sleeper train car that Union Pacific constructed specifically for Halbrook and his teammates. The special attention paid off, as Swede broke the school single-season scoring record in his first varsity season. He learned to shoot hook shots with both hands and improved his jump shot. Despite his lack of foot speed, Halbrook was well coordinated, and he improved rapidly.

In his second varsity season, Halbrook was an All-American, averaging 21 points and 13 rebounds in leading Oregon State to the Pacific Coast Conference Title. In the NCAA West Regionals, they lost to eventual champion San Francisco by a single point. But that was the end of Halbrook's college days.

Swede had been in and out of trouble academically since arriving at college and at one point was suspended from the team for cutting classes. As one faculty member told *Sports Illustrated,* "None of us could ever recall having seen Wade smile. Life seems to be a pretty grim business with him."

Halbrook left college to join the Wichita Vickers of the National Industrial Basketball League, where he played for five years before entering the NBA as a twenty-seven-year-old rookie. If he had ever possessed the stuff to make it in the NBA, he no longer did. Two years later he was out of the NBA.

The name Swede Halbrook resurfaced in the sports pages in May 1988, when his obituary appeared in newspapers around the country. Swede had died of a heart attack while riding a metropolitan bus in Portland. At the age of fifty-five, the 7′3″ giant had been earning his living as a construction worker.

How Dan Issel Had to Leave Kentucky

Dan Issel played sixteen years of pro basketball, eleven of them in Denver. But if Issel had gotten his way, he would have played his whole career in Kentucky.

A native of Batavia, Illinois, Issel was a 6′9″ All-American at the University of Kentucky in 1970, and certain to be a first-round choice in the pro drafts. The ABA held its draft first, with Issel selected by Dallas. Issel said that the only way he would play in the ABA was if Louisville had a franchise. And almost before you could sing "My Old Kentucky Home," Louisville had a team, the Kentucky Colonels, and had acquired the rights to Issel.

Dan was so eager to stay in Kentucky that he signed a five-year contract for less than $500,000 before the NBA had even held their draft. His quick decision undoubtedly cost him a lot of money that could have been won in a bidding war.

Issel was an immediate hit in the ABA. He averaged almost 30 points a game to lead the league in scoring, and shared Rookie-of-the-Year honors with Virginia's Charlie Scott. After the season, according to Issel, the Phoenix Suns offered to triple his salary if he would jump to the NBA. But again, he ignored the lure of big bucks because of his love for the state of Kentucky. Eventually, though, not even that love could keep Issel in the Bluegrass State.

In 1975, Issel and the Kentucky Colonels won their first ABA title. As it turned out, it would also be their last. Despite the championship, the Colonels were losing a lot of money. On September 19, Colonels owner John Y. Brown decided to sell Issel to the new Baltimore team for a reported $350,000 and a player named Tom Owen. Issel was crushed, and he could have used his no-trade clause to block the deal. But it looked like the Kentucky franchise wasn't going to

Kentucky's Dan Issel

survive, so he reluctantly complied with the trade.

Issel's new team, the Baltimore Claws, was actually the bankrupt Memphis Tams franchise, which had been sold to new owners. Issel spent all of ten days in Baltimore before his career as a Claw abruptly came to an end. The Baltimore owners were badly underfinanced and had not sent the money they owed for Issel to John Y. Brown in Kentucky. So Brown arranged for Issel to be traded again, this time from Baltimore to Denver, for Dave Robisch and a large amount of cash. The money bypassed Baltimore completely, since they had never paid Kentucky for Issel. Denver sent the cash directly to Kentucky, and Dan Issel became a Nugget.

Issel had been in Baltimore long enough to receive one paycheck. You guessed it—the check bounced. The Claws played only three exhibition games and folded before the season began, without ever playing an official ABA game.

And Dan Issel? He played one year with Denver in the ABA and ten more with the Nuggets in the NBA. When he retired in 1985, he ranked fourth on the all-time pro basketball scoring list. Issel scored over 27,000 points. But it's a safe bet that he would have traded in half of them for the chance to play his whole career in Kentucky.

The Tightest Scoring Race in NBA History

Decided on April 9, 1978, the final day of the season, the race between David Thompson of Denver and George Gervin of San Antonio produced two of the NBA's greatest offensive performances, with both of them coming on the road.

Thompson and the Nuggets were in Detroit, and it became immediately clear that the Denver team would do all it could to help Thompson win the title. David made the most of their assistance, going on a first-quarter rampage for 32 points, an NBA record for one quarter. At halftime, Thompson had a total of 53 and had hit 20 of 23 shots from the floor. He cooled off somewhat in the second half, hitting only 8 of 15 shots and netting 20 points, for a game total of 73 points.

Thompson's total was the third highest in NBA history, and more than anyone other than Wilt Chamberlain has ever scored. An appreciative Thompson thanked his teammates, saying, "They got me the ball and I was hitting. Everything was going for me in the first half. I couldn't keep up the pace in the second half, though, I got a little tired."

The Nuggets lost the game, 139–137, and Thompson felt bad about losing. But he left the arena thinking he had won the NBA scoring title as he had trailed Gervin by only a few hundredths of a point. Gervin, however, had other ideas. When he and the San Antonio Spurs took the court at the New Orleans Superdome that night against the Jazz, Gervin knew that he needed 58 points to overtake Thompson and win the scoring title. No problem. Despite the Jazz doing everything they could to stop him, "the Iceman" came close to that total in the first half alone.

He scored 20 points in the first quarter, then shattered Thompson's one-quarter record, which had lasted all of seven hours, by pumping in 33 in the second quarter. Gervin's 53-point first half duplicated Thompson's performance and removed all suspense from the race. With ten minutes left in the third quarter, Gervin hit for points #58 and #59, locking up the title. Coach Doug Moe removed Gervin from the game, to a standing ovation. And when he returned eight minutes later, his teammates no longer tried to feed him. Gervin finished with 63 points as the Spurs lost, 153–132.

The final scoring averages were Gervin 27.22, Thompson 27.15, a difference of just seven hundredths of a point. And while this was to be the first of four scoring titles won by Gervin, Thompson never got this close again. Gervin and Thompson were named as the two guards on the 1978 NBA All-Star Team, another honor that Thompson was never able to repeat. But his 73-point game lives on as part of the most exciting scoring race ever.

THE SCORING LINES OF 4/9/78

	Min.	FGM	FGA	FTM	FTA	Reb.	Ast.	PF	Pts.
Thompson	43	28	38	17	20	7	2	2	73
Gervin	33	23	49	17	20	2	1	3	63

The Breaking of the NBA Color Line

The color line in major-league baseball was broken by Jackie Robinson in 1947. But in the late 1940s, the only potential employer for a black basketball star coming out of college was the Harlem Globetrotters. Ironically, some have claimed that Globetrotters owner Abe Saperstein helped delay the breaking of the NBA color line.

They charge that to protect his monopoly on the great black players, Saperstein threatened to stop bringing the Globetrotters into NBA arenas as preliminaries to NBA games if the league were to become integrated. Such a boycott by Saperstein would have denied many thousands of dollars to NBA clubs who drew additional fans when the Globetrotters were part of the attraction.

The age of opportunity for blacks in basketball finally arrived in 1950, when Boston Celtics owner Walter Brown used his second draft choice to select 6′5″ Chuck Cooper out of Duquesne University. While he was a freshman at Duquesne, the University of Tennessee had refused to play a scheduled game unless Duquesne guaranteed that Cooper would not play. One month later, the University of Miami had canceled a game scheduled against Duquesne at the Orange Bowl, pointing to an antiquated city ordinance that prohibited blacks and whites from playing in the same game.

This type of racial discrimination continued at some colleges long after the NBA became integrated. As late as 1962, Southeastern Conference champion Mississippi State turned down an NCAA tournament bid, refusing to play against teams with black players.

But in the NBA, the Celtics' drafting of Cooper opened the door for other owners to end the segregation on their teams. In the eighth round, the Washington Capitols drafted another black player, Earl Lloyd of West Virginia State. Shortly thereafter, the New York Knicks purchased the contract of star center Nat "Sweetwater" Clifton from the Globetrotters for a reported $25,000.

Nicknamed the "Big Cat," 6′6″ center Earl Lloyd became the first black player to play in the NBA, because Washington opened the season before the Celtics and Knicks did. October 31, 1950, the night Lloyd officially broke the NBA color line, remains a landmark date in the history of professional basketball.

Chuck Cooper, the first black NBA draftee

But Chuck Cooper is the man who most consider the Jackie Robinson of basketball, perhaps because of the widely publicized prejudice he encountered in college. More likely, it's because it was the Celtics' drafting of Cooper that was comparable to the Dodgers' signing of Robinson, making Boston's Walter Brown the Branch Rickey of the NBA.

Some NBA owners continued to refrain from signing blacks, feeling that many of their fans would disapprove. Some longtime observers contend that until the 1960s, there was an unwritten rule that teams would restrict themselves to three black players per team, then five per team in the early '60s. Whether or not those agreements existed, the NBA's first three blacks all performed capably.

Cooper averaged 9 points a game for the Celtics in his rookie year. He went on to play six years in the NBA, four of them with Boston, but never equaled the point production of his rookie season. He retired with a career average of 6.7 points a game.

Lloyd played in only seven games for the Washington Capitols before being drafted into the military. By the time he returned to the league in 1952, the Washington team had disbanded, so Lloyd joined the Syracuse Nationals and played nine years in the league, averaging around 8 points and 7 rebounds. Lloyd was the starting center for Syracuse when they won the NBA title in 1955.

Of the three black pioneers, Lloyd was the only one to win a league championship. He was later named coach of the Detroit Pistons, and in 1972 became the first black coach to be fired by an NBA team. Ironically, his successor, Ray Scott, became the first black coach to succeed another.

Nat Clifton never won an NBA title and never coached in the league, but of the three, he is probably best remembered. Nicknamed Sweetwater because of his affection for Coke and 7-Up, Clifton was already a star when he entered the NBA. At the age of twenty-eight, he was the Harlem Globetrotters' leading scorer in 1950 when the Knicks purchased him for a reported $25,000. Clifton later claimed that he and Globetrotters owner Abe Saperstein had a dispute over money, and that Nat was planning to leave the team when Saperstein found out and decided to sell his contract.

Although listed as 6′7″, Clifton was probably closer to 6′5″, but he rebounded with much taller men. Nat was a superlative passer whose all-around talents helped take the Knicks all the way to the NBA finals in his rookie season. Clifton did not shoot much in the NBA, concentrating instead on defense and rebounding, but he managed to average 10 points a game in his seven-year NBA career.

"Sweetwater" was thirty-five years old when he left the NBA to join the Harlem Magicians, a team started by former Globetrotters Goose Tatum and Marques Haynes. He laughed it up with them for four years before a bad knee forced him to quit. Clifton returned to his hometown of Chicago with a lifetime full of memories as one of basketball's true pioneers.

Rhode Island's "Race-Horse" Basketball

The first college basketball teams sprang up in 1893, just over a year after the game was invented. The first university to take on an outside opponent was the University of Toronto, which defeated the Toronto YMCA 2–1 in January of 1893. Then in February, Vanderbilt fielded the first college team in the United States, as they beat the Nashville YMCA in a high-scoring affair, 9–6. (Those Commodores could shoot!) These teams each had nine players on the court, but four years later, in 1897, the rule was changed to the present-day five-man squads. In the first game under the new rule, Yale defeated Pennsylvania 32–10.

Clearly the game was opening up, and teams in different parts of the country soon developed different styles of play. By 1904, Eastern teams preferred lots of dribbling, short passes underneath, and tough defense. Midwestern clubs favored longer passes along with an equally tight defense. And in the far West, they played an early version of "run and gun," with everyone streaking the length of the floor.

In the 1920s, college basketball teams were scoring about 30 points per game, sometimes even less. At Rhode Island State College, coach Frank Keaney devised a new style to allow his undermanned team to compete against larger schools. In 1928, he began teaching his team a strategy using long passes, fast breaks, and more frequent shooting, combined with a pressing defense. He waited two years to introduce it into intercollegiate play, then unveiled it in 1930.

Keaney's new style was scoffed at by other coaches, who called it "fire-engine" and "race-horse" basketball. But it worked. Rhode Island produced the country's first point-a-minute team, averaging 40 points a game. And they kept upping their point totals in the ensuing years. Fans loved the freewheeling style, and soon it was adopted by coaches at other schools.

Low-scoring basketball was becoming a thing of the past, and in 1937–38, the rules were changed to eliminate the center jump after each basket. With play speeded up considerably, everyone's point totals leaped, and Rhode Island averaged 71 points a game. Basketball was beginning to look like the game of today.

The Self-Made Superstar

At 6′9″ and only 215 pounds, Bob Pettit was thought by many to be too skinny to make it in the NBA, even after he averaged 30 points a game in his senior year at Louisiana State University. They said that Pettit did not jump well enough and seemed awkward. But the Milwaukee Hawks drafted him in the first round in 1954, planning to shift him from center, where he played at LSU, to a corner position.

Pettit immediately went to work at learning the unfamiliar position. He developed new moves he could use while facing the basket, to free himself for the jump shot that he rarely missed. He underwent a weight-training program to strengthen himself for the long, arduous pro season. When he entered the NBA, he was ready.

Pettit won the NBA Rookie of the Year Award and was a first-team All-Star, averaging 20 points and 14 rebounds in his first year. The Hawks moved to St. Louis the next year, and Pettit led the league in scoring and rebounding, a feat that earned him the NBA's Most Valuable Player Award.

Bob went on to play eleven years in the NBA, all of them with the Hawks. In each of his first ten years, he finished in the top five in the league in scoring and rebounding, a streak that ended in his final season because of an injury that limited him to 50 games. He was a first-team All-Star ten years in a row, and a second-team All-Star in his last season. He won the MVP Award twice, and was the All-Star Game MVP four times. And he was at his best in the playoffs, leading the Hawks to their only NBA title in 1958, when he scored 50 points in the sixth and deciding game.

Pettit was a master of position play, and used finesse to become a great rebounder. His jump shot was the best of its era in the NBA. When Bob retired in 1965, he was the NBA's all-time leading scorer, with a career average of 26.4 points and 16.1 rebounds a game. It was an incredible achievement for a player who had been cut from his high-school team.

As a kid growing up in Baton Rouge, Robert E. Lee Pettit was so awkward that he couldn't make his church league team. He was cut from the high-school team as a sophomore, but then spent hundreds of hours shooting at a basket in his backyard. He made the high-school team the next year and continued to improve throughout his high-school and college career.

When Pettit retired from the NBA to become a banker, he looked back on those boyhood days, recalling an entire season at age eleven when he hadn't scored a single point. But he more than made up for it by becoming the first man in pro basketball to score 20,000 of them.

Scoring machine Bob Pettit

Dare to Dribble!

James Naismith's original thirteen rules of basketball, first published in January 1892, included the prohibition of "traveling." Those rules stipulate that there is to be no running with the ball. Furthermore, the player has to throw the ball from the spot on which he catches it.

But what about dribbling? Naismith made no mention of it.

It didn't take long for basketball players to attempt to get around the rule against running with the ball. They started by introducing the pivot, that is, keeping one foot planted while moving the other one around. In 1893, less than two years after the first game was played, the pivot became officially permissible.

The next step was the use of the dribble, a technique first used extensively to move the ball by Yale University in 1896. Rules were soon passed restricting this maneuver.

The double dribble (dribbling, stopping, and then dribbling again) was outlawed in 1898, and dribbling with two hands was made illegal as well. In 1901, a rule was instituted prohibiting the dribbler from taking a shot. If you dribbled the ball, you had to pass it when you finished dribbling. This rule stayed around until 1915, when other restrictions on dribbling were introduced.

Once it was determined that a player dribbling the ball should be allowed to shoot, the rules were changed to limit dribbling to just one bounce. (You certainly couldn't go very far with the ball under that legislation.) Many coaches believed that teams should be able to move the ball into position for a good shot by passing the ball, which was, after all, Naismith's original idea.

In 1929, the Joint Committee of the National Association of Basketball Coaches met to discuss the controversial issue of dribbling. The top professional team, the Celtics, were known for their passing, not their dribbling. But Celtics star Nat Holman, who was also the coach at City College in New York, convinced the college coaches that college players should not be expected to pass the ball the way the Celtics do. Holman helped persuade them to let their players dribble, and hoopsters have been bouncing the ball freely ever since.

There must have been a special beauty in seeing the early teams whip the ball around without the benefit of continuous dribbling. But it's also hard to imagine the game being very exciting to watch without the possibility of a Magic Johnson going coast-to-coast with the ball.

The Unlikely Looking Star

Imagine the sight of an NBA forward only 6′4″ tall, wheezing and gulping for air as he runs up and down the court—a man who seems to be panting. You would probably have a hard time taking him seriously as an offensive threat. That is, unless that player was Paul Arizin of the Philadelphia Warriors.

One of the great scorers of the 1950s, Arizin had a sinus condition that caused him to cough and gasp for air on the court, but it never bothered his shooting.

Paul Arizin spent 10 years in the NBA.

The man they called Pitching Paul averaged over 22 points a game during his ten-year NBA career, and twice he led the league in scoring. He was the fifth man in NBA history to score 10,000 points, and he reached that lofty figure faster than any man before him.

Arizin helped the Warriors win the NBA championship in 1956 and played in nine NBA All-Star Games. He accomplished all this despite missing two years early in his career while serving in the US Marines.

From start to finish, Arizin's career was an unusual story. Unlike most pro basketball players, Paul did not play for his high-school team, competing instead in Philadelphia's church leagues. He attended Villanova without a scholarship and didn't go out for their team, either. But Arizin became so well known in the recreational leagues that Villanova coach Al Severance invited him to join the Wildcats. Arizin proceeded to lead the team in scoring as a sophomore; as a senior two years later he led the nation with a 26-point average.

Arizin became the first-round draft choice of the hometown Philadelphia Warriors, and quickly showed that he could score against NBA forwards who were usually three to four inches taller than he was. He did it with one of the first great jump shots in the NBA, a line-drive jumper that he had developed accidentally on the slippery floors of low-ceilinged church gymnasiums. Arizin also had great timing and anticipation, and despite his breathing problem, he was one of the league's best leapers and a fine rebounder.

When the Warriors moved to San Francisco in 1962, Arizin was still at the top of his game. But he decided not to go west with the team, choosing instead to stay in Philadelphia and play in the minors in the Eastern League. Not surprisingly, he proceeded to win its MVP award.

The Spectacular Rookie Season of Elgin Baylor

Regarded by many as the greatest forward ever to play the game, Elgin Baylor first learned his moves on the courts of Washington, DC. Even in high school, he displayed the remarkable body control that made his drives to the basket unlike those of any player before him. He could hang in the air longer and shoot better from an off-balance position than anyone else. But despite these skills, Baylor almost missed his chance to play college basketball.

In high school Elgin was not a good student. He dropped out for a while and worked in a furniture store, playing basketball at night for fun. Baylor returned to high school and graduated, but not with the type of grades that would enable him to enter most colleges. A friend arranged for him to attend the College of Idaho on a football scholarship. But the Idaho football coach, Sam Vokes, was also the basketball coach, and Elgin soon found himself back on the court.

Baylor averaged 31 points a game in his first year, but then the school fired Vokes and cut back on scholarships, leading Elgin to transfer to Seattle University. After sitting out the required year, Baylor had two big years at Seattle, averaging 30 and then 32 points a game and leading the Chieftains to the NCAA finals in 1958. Although Baylor had 25 points and 19 rebounds in the championship game, Seattle lost to Kentucky, 84–72.

The Minneapolis Lakers, the NBA's worst team, drafted Baylor in the first round, and the 6′5″ forward became a franchise saver. Laker president Bob Short later said that had Baylor not signed, the club would have gone bankrupt. As it turned out, Elgin was just what the doctor ordered for the Lakers' ailing franchise.

Baylor took a team that had gone 19–53 the year before and led them all the way to the NBA finals, where they were beaten four straight by the Celtics. Baylor averaged 24.9 points (fourth in the league), 15 rebounds (third in the league), and 4 assists, made the All-NBA first team, won the Rookie of the Year Award, and was co-MVP of the All-Star Game.

In one game he pumped in 55 points, the third-highest total in NBA history. But that was just the beginning of the NBA scoring heroics turned in by Elgin Baylor, a man who became an instant superstar in professional basketball.

Instant superstar Elgin Baylor

Baylor's Single-Game Scoring Records

The Celtics had beaten the Lakers 21 straight times in regular season play, but early in Elgin Baylor's second season, he and his teammates gained a measure of revenge. On November 8, 1959, the Lakers hosted the Celtics at the Minneapolis Auditorium and blew the league champions right out of the building. The Lakers built up a 30-point lead in the third quarter and went on to win 136–115. But the big story was not the Lakers' victory but rather the part that Elgin Baylor played.

Baylor scored 64 points, breaking the NBA record of 63* points set by Joe

Fulks of Philadelphia back in 1949. Elgin sank 25 out of 47 field goal attempts and was 14 of 19 from the free throw line. His record-breaking bucket came on a ten-foot driving jumper with just thirty-one seconds to go.

Baylor owned the NBA single-game scoring record, but it would last for only fifty-three weeks. When it was shattered, the man who broke it was Elgin Baylor himself. On November 15, 1960, exactly one year and one week after his 64-point spree, Baylor fired in 71 points in a game against the Knicks. This time, Baylor's explosion came on the road, at Madison Square Garden, and this time it was for the Los Angeles Lakers, who had moved from Minneapolis in the off-season.

Many of Baylor's 28 field goals came on his patented drives, several of them from seemingly impossible angles. Elgin scored 34 points in the first half, and when the Lakers led by 17 going into the fourth quarter, teammate Jerry West and company began feeding him the ball at every opportunity.

Baylor broke his 64-point record with 1:35 remaining, and when he finally left the court, the Garden crowd stood and cheered for almost a minute. The Knicks had lost 123–108, but the crowd had seen a performance they would never forget.

Wilt Chamberlain came along and broke Baylor's 71-point record a couple of years later. But other than Wilt, the only player in NBA history to score more points in a single game than Elgin Baylor is David Thompson, the high-flying Denver Nugget.

The College Basketball Scandal of 1951

The most devastating blow that basketball has ever suffered hit home in January 1951, when Junius Kellogg, the sophomore center for Manhattan College, was offered $1,000 to help fix a game against De Paul. Instead of taking the bribe, Kellogg pretended to be interested, informed his coach Kenneth Norton, and helped trap the people involved.

Manhattan won the game 62–59. Several hours later the police arrested five men on bribery and conspiracy charges—three gamblers and two of Kellogg's teammates. One of the players, Henry Poppe, quickly confessed to fixing several games over the previous two seasons, leading to a major investigation by Manhattan District Attorney Frank Hogan.

By the time Hogan and the grand jury completed their work in 1953, more than thirty-two players from seven schools had been arrested. They were charged with conspiring to fix the scores of close to 100 games in twenty-three cities in seventeen different states over a span of four seasons. Generally, the players had not been asked to lose the games intentionally, but rather to win by fewer points than the point spread.

Four of the seven schools involved were from New York City, including the 1950 City College team that had won the NCAA tournament and the NIT, beating Bradley University in both finals. All five starters from City College were arrested, and so were three of the Bradley players.

Kentucky coach Adolph Rupp declared, "They couldn't touch our boys with a ten-foot pole." But when the dust had cleared, Kentucky appeared to be one of the worst offenders, as their All-Americans Alex Groza and Ralph Beard were among those arrested.

In the end, a total of twenty players were found guilty of throwing games or fixing points. A few of them went to jail, but most received suspended sentences. The convicted gamblers, however, were imprisoned.

Most of the players were thrown out of school. Some were readmitted but not allowed to play intercollegiate sports. And the players involved were banned for life from the NBA, including Groza and Beard, who had already become NBA stars. Long Island University star Sherman White, considered the best player in the country in 1951, had to settle for playing his pro ball in the minor-league Eastern League.

City College and Long Island University decided to drop basketball from their athletic programs for a while. Kentucky had to sit out a one-year suspension imposed by the NCAA. But the other four schools involved—Manhattan, NYU, Bradley, and Toledo—continued their programs.

The scandal was a stunning blow to college basketball, especially at Madison Square Garden, where many schools complied with a boycott of the arena called for by the NCAA. The NBA received a giant boost, as many of the fans began to shift their attention to the pros. And, although the college game survived, it has never recovered the hold it had at the Garden in New York.

But the scandal might never have happened if college presidents and coaches had read the warning signs correctly.

As early as 1943, there were some obvious signs that gambling on college basketball was becoming dangerous to the game. In the NIT that year, a spectator ran out on the Madison Square Garden court and kissed a Utah player who had made a last-second basket against Kentucky. While Kentucky won the game easily, the Utah basket cut the winning margin to 8 points, beneath the ten-point spread that gamblers had established. Reportedly, the kissing gambler made $15,000 on that otherwise inconsequential shot.

In 1944, Utah coach Vadal Peterson flattened a gambler who had gone to the coach's hotel room and asked, "How much would it cost to have Utah lose to Dartmouth in the NCAA final?" Peterson's verbal response was unprintable, but the attempt should have caused far greater concern than it actually did. Hall-of-Famer Phog Allen, who was coaching at Kansas, declared that college presidents needed to hire an absolute czar to rule over college sports. If not, he warned, "Some of these college boys who have never seen big money are going to sell out and it will cause a scandal that will stink to high heaven."

In January of 1945 there was another indication that Allen's prophecy was correct. New York police were keeping tabs on a suspected garment thief named Henry Rosen. They observed two young men, Bernard Barnett and Larry Pearlstein, entering his house and decided to confront them, thinking they might also be thieves. Barnett and Pearlstein were basketball players, not garment thieves, but quickly panicked when the police arrived. They admitted that Rosen had paid them $1,000 to divide among themselves and three other members of the Brooklyn College basketball team.

Rosen was to tell them later how their upcoming game against Akron University was to turn out. The Akron team traveled over 700 miles for the game, which was canceled by the time they arrived. Three other Brooklyn players had confessed to taking money from gamblers, and all five of them were expelled from school. (It was later learned that Pearlstein had never registered as a student in the first place!)

The players were not brought up on criminal charges, but Rosen and an accomplice were convicted of conspiracy to cheat and defraud, sentenced to one year in the state penitentiary, and fined $500.

In 1949, a George Washington University player reported a bribe attempt leading to an arrest and conviction of four gamblers. But these were all seen as isolated events, rather than as indications of the major scandal that Allen had foreseen, and which exploded into the headlines in 1951. Perhaps if Allen's words had been heeded, college basketball's blackest days could have been avoided.

The Celtics' First NBA Championship

Despite the presence of All-Star guards Bob Cousy and Bill Sharman, the Boston Celtics had never made it to the NBA finals before the 1956–57 season, when Bill Russell arrived to give the team the rebounding it had always lacked. Another rookie helped the Celtics cause that year as well, 6′7″ forward Tommy Heinsohn, who won the Rookie of the Year Award.

With their frontcourt revamped, Red Auerbach's Celtics romped to an easy Eastern Division crown and a sweep of Syracuse in the playoff semifinals. In the

Red Auerbach

final round they would face a St. Louis Hawks team that had finished in a three-way tie for first in the West—but with a losing record. And ironically, it was St. Louis who had traded the draft rights to Russell to the Celtics for Ed Macauley and Cliff Hagan.

The Celtics were heavily favored, but coach Alex Hannum's Hawks shocked everyone by winning Game One in Boston in double overtime. Boston came back to lead the series, three games to two, but the Hawks won Game Six in St. Louis by two points, to set up a decisive seventh game at the Boston Garden. Feelings were running so high that after one of the games, Celtics coach Red Auerbach punched Hawks owner Ben Kerner.

On April 13, 1957, a capacity crowd of 13,909 jammed the Boston Garden for Game Seven and witnessed one of the greatest basketball games of all time. A more dramatic game had never been played, as the lead changed hands twenty times. On six occasions, the Celtics opened up a lead only to have the Hawks storm back. At the end of regulation time, Hawks forward Bob Pettit sank two free throws to send it into overtime. In the overtime, the Celtics again had the lead with time running out, but Jack Coleman of the Hawks hit a one-hander to force a second overtime.

Finally, in the second overtime, a twenty-footer by Frank Ramsey put Boston ahead to stay, and a last second shot by Pettit, which would have forced another overtime, went off the rim. The final score: Boston 125, St. Louis 123.

Pettit had been sensational in defeat, with 39 points. Heinsohn had poured in 37 for Boston, easily overshadowing his 7 consecutive missed free throws. St. Louis guard Slater Martin scored 23 points and played the entire fifty-eight minutes.

And Russell? He scored 19 points and pulled down 32 rebounds to lead the Celtics to their first championship. It was a script that would repeat itself year after year, as Boston won 11 championships in a span of 12 years, but not until the Hawks got even the following season.

The City College Cinderella Team of 1950

Only once in basketball history has the same team won the NCAA and the NIT tournaments in the same year. This feat was pulled off in 1950 by the Beavers of City College in an amazing story that ended in disgrace.

When the regular season ended in 1950, City College was 17–5, good enough to get an invitation to the NIT at Madison Square Garden, but not as one of the four seeded teams in the twelve-team field. They proceeded to destroy defending champion San Francisco and second-seeded Kentucky on their way to the final, where they would face the Bradley Braves, the number-one team in the land. The Beavers had only one experienced player, captain Irwin Dambrot, while Bradley was led by All-Americans Gene Melchiorre and Paul Unruh.

Bradley jumped out to a 29–18 lead, but City College roared back to win 69–61 as Dambrot pumped in 23 points before a hometown crowd of 18,000. The NCAA tourney, which began the next night, would also have its finale at the Garden. The same two teams arrived at that party, exactly ten days after the NIT final.

Intent on avenging their defeat in the NIT, Bradley nonetheless fell behind early this time, trailing by 7 at halftime and by 11 with ten minutes to go. But the Braves turned on a ferocious full-court press and closed the gap to a single point with forty seconds left. Then, with fifteen seconds left, Melchiorre took the ball to the hoop and Dambrot made the play of the game. The Beavers captain stripped the ball away from Melchiorre, then arched a long pass downcourt that led to an easy layup. City College had a 71–68 victory and a sweep of the post-season tournaments.

With Dambrot the only graduating senior in the City College starting lineup and four sophomore starters returning, Beaver fans had visions of a dynasty. But in February 1951, all four returnees were arrested and confessed to fixing points in several games the year before. City College canceled their final two games of the season, and later that year, a total of seven members of the national championship team officially pleaded guilty to conspiracy charges. They had actually shaved points in several games during their championship season. Now they would have to pay for it.

All seven players were banned from ever playing in the NBA. One of them, Floyd Layne, was considered a "can't-miss" pro prospect. When he was arrested, Layne showed detectives a flowerpot in his bedroom, where almost $2,900 in bribe money was embedded in the dirt.

City College was only one of seven teams involved in the stunning scandal. But when the busts were made, it was the defending champions who had the most to lose—and did.

The "Garbageman"

In today's basketball jargon, we would call him a "power forward" and a great "offensive rebounder." But in the '60s, Bailey Howell was considered a "garbageman," and he was proud of it. The man who had the knack of being in position to tap in countless missed shots frequently pointed out that his shortest shots were the hardest points to get.

At 6′7″ and 220 pounds, Bailey Howell played hard, a model of determination and durability for twelve years in the NBA. His devotion to the game began in his hometown of Middleton, Tennessee, where basketball was a year-round game. Howell made the high-school team as a seventh grader, and eventually left the state to play college basketball for Mississippi State, where coach Babe McCarthy built his offense around Bailey.

In those years, Kentucky was the powerhouse of the Southeast Conference, but with Howell, Mississippi State could challenge the Wildcats. In his junior and senior years, Howell averaged 28 points a game, including 27 points in a win over Kentucky that gave his team the SEC championship in 1959. Unfortunately, the rest of the nation would not find out about Howell in the NCAA tournament, as Mississippi State refused to play against integrated teams, allowing Kentucky to represent the conference.

Howell was drafted in the first round by Detroit, where he played his first five NBA seasons. He moved on to Baltimore for two years, then finally got the break of his career in 1966 when he was acquired by the Boston Celtics.

When the Celtics sent seven-foot center Mel Counts to the Bullets for Howell, they hoped Bailey could replace high-scoring forward Tommy Heinsohn, who had just retired, as both a scorer and rebounder. Howell had a career average of 20 points a game, but he was already twenty-nine years old, and some thought he might have lost a step.

Instead, Howell raised his level of play on joining the Celtics. He still scored 20 points a game, and he helped out Bill Russell under the boards. Although Boston lost the NBA championship to Philadelphia in 1967, they regained the title in 1968. In that year's finals, Howell was a major contributor. In the sixth and deciding game against the Lakers, the thirty-one-year-old Howell scored 30

Bailey Howell, a model of determination

points and had 11 rebounds.

The Celtics won the title again in 1969, with Howell again playing a major role. Howell was typical of the kind of veteran the Celtics always seemed to come up with to help them win. As Red Auerbach said about Howell, "He's been a Celtic all his life. It just took him a lot longer to get the uniform." He was also the man who made the term "garbageman" one of admiration around the NBA.

Houston Snaps UCLA's 47-Game Win Streak

Entering the 1967–68 season, John Wooden's UCLA Bruins were the defending NCAA champions, having finished the previous year with an undefeated record in their first season with Lew Alcindor at center. They appeared destined to repeat that achievement as they won the first 13 games of Alcindor's second year.

But on January 20, 1968, the Bruins ran into another undefeated team, the Houston Cougars, and another phenomenal center, Elvin "the Big E" Hayes. Coach Guy Lewis's Cougars entered the game ranked second in the nation behind UCLA, with a 16–0 record. Houston's last loss had been to the Bruins, 73–58, in the NCAA semifinals in Louisville the year before.

This time, however, the Cougars had the home crowd on their side; 52,693 fans packed the Astrodome, which was hosting a basketball game for the first time. The wooden basketball floor had to be shipped in from the Los Angeles Sports Arena, at a cost of $10,000, because the Astrodome did not even own a basketball floor.

As the game began, UCLA sported a 47-game winning streak, 13 games shy of the record set by Bill Russell's University of San Francisco team in the mid-50s. But they knew going in that Alcindor might not be at his best, having missed the previous two games with an eye injury.

As it turned out, not only was the big guy not at his best, he had the worst night of his collegiate career. The combination of a subpar game by Alcindor and a stupendous performance by Hayes enabled Houston to upset UCLA, but just barely. Sparked by Hayes's 29-point first half, Houston led at halftime 46–43. They maintained a narrow lead for most of the second half, but with forty-four seconds to go, a basket by UCLA guard Lucius Allen tied it 69–69.

Houston brought the ball down and got it to Hayes, who was fouled and calmly dropped in the two free throws to put Houston back on top, 71–69. UCLA had one last chance but threw the ball out of bounds without getting off a shot.

The Bruins were clearly done in by bad shooting. They hit only 34% from the field, while Houston sank 46% of their field goal attempts. Led by guards George Reynolds and Don Chaney, the Cougars did an outstanding job in handling UCLA's famed press. But ultimately it was the Alcindor-Hayes matchup that decided the outcome.

Alcindor scored just 15 points, hitting just 4 out of 18 shots from the floor. Hayes erupted for 39 points, sinking 17 of 25 from the floor. Hayes outrebounded Alcindor, 15–12, blocked three of Lew's shots, and stole the ball from him twice. And "the Big E" did all this despite playing the last eleven minutes with four fouls. Hayes had outscored Alcindor 39–15, and Houston had won 71–69, in claiming the number-one ranking in the nation.

Houston had snapped the UCLA streak, but it didn't take long for the Bruins to avenge the defeat. The two teams hooked up again in the NCAA semifinals, ironically played at the Los Angeles Sports Arena. Although the floor was the same, the outcome was vastly different.

Hayes battles Alcindor.

UCLA Avenges Loss by Destroying Houston

Houston's memorable 71–69 win over UCLA at the Astrodome on January 20, 1968, which snapped the Bruins' 47-game winning streak, is remembered by all who witnessed it. Somewhat forgotten is the ease with which UCLA avenged that loss by destroying the Cougars later that year.

The rematch came in the NCAA semifinals at the Los Angeles Sports Arena, the same floor that had been shipped to Houston for the Cougars' win over the Bruins. That win over the national champions had spurred Houston to an undefeated season, with 32 straight wins dating back to their loss to UCLA in the NCAA semifinals the previous year. Houston center Elvin Hayes, who had outscored UCLA's Lew Alcindor 39–15 in leading the Cougars to victory at the Astrodome, had averaged almost 38 points a game and was the Player of the Year in college basketball.

Alcindor though, was recovering from an eye injury when the Cougars beat the Bruins, and was way off his game. As UCLA got ready for the rematch, coach John Wooden installed a special defense designed to deny Hayes the basketball.

Guy Lewis, on the losing end this time

It was a diamond-and-one, with Alcindor playing closest to the basket in the four-man diamond-shaped zone, and forward Lynn Shackelford shadowing Hayes wherever he went. UCLA's strategy worked so well that the game turned out to be one of the biggest mismatches in the history of the Final Four.

On March 22, 1968, with Houston ranked number-one in the nation and UCLA rated second, they got set for their rematch, an NCAA semifinal game. This time the Bruins had the home crowd on their side as 15,742 fans packed the Sports Arena. UCLA was determined to avenge what had been their only loss of the season, and they did it in convincing fashion.

The Bruins controlled the game from the opening tap and completely annihilated the Cougars. Their defense kept the ball away from Hayes so effectively that "the Big E" was held to only 10 points. Meanwhile, Alcindor scored 19, as did his teammates Lucius Allen and Mike Lynn.

UCLA led at halftime 53–31, and late in the game they opened up a gigantic 44-point lead. Wooden then began removing his starters from the game, one at a time. When Alcindor was taken out he held up his arm, pointing with his index finger. The message was unmistakable: UCLA was number-one. Who could see it any other way? The final score made it clear: UCLA 101, Houston 69.

Houston coach Guy Lewis summed it up by saying, "That was the greatest exhibition of basketball I've ever seen in my life. They could have beaten anybody—I mean anybody."

The next night, UCLA made their national championship official by polishing off North Carolina 78–55 to win the title for the second year in a row. In the minds of most fans, they had already won it the night before by thrashing Houston and "the Big E."

Hawks Turn Tables on Celtics to Win First Title

The year after Boston's 1957 double-overtime win over St. Louis in the seventh game of the NBA finals, Bill Russell was the league's MVP and top rebounder, while teammate Bob Cousy led in assists for the seventh straight year. But Hawks forward Bob Pettit was third in scoring and second in rebounding. And Pettit stole the show in the NBA All-Star Game with 28 points and 26 rebounds.

Not surprisingly, the Celtics and Hawks made it to the finals again with ease, each winning their division by a margin of eight games. Boston disposed of Philadelphia four games to one in the Eastern Division finals, holding the Warriors under 100 points in every game. The Hawks, meanwhile, polished off Detroit 4–1, winning the last two games by a total of 68 points. The Hawks had never won the NBA title, but this time they would not be denied.

The 1958 NBA finals began exactly as they had the previous year, with the Hawks upsetting the Celtics in Game One at the Boston Garden. After four games, they were again tied at two apiece. But in Game Three, Russell suffered an ankle injury that severely limited his mobility and his playing time for the rest of the series.

The Hawks took advantage of Russell's injury to win Game Five in Boston, out-rebounding the Celtics by a wide margin on the way to a 102–100 victory. That gave the Hawks a chance to win it all at home in Game Six.

Never has a star risen to the occasion more gloriously than did Bob Pettit in that sixth game. Pettit set an NBA playoff game record with a whopping 50 points. The Hawks needed every one of them, as they held off the Celtics 110–109 to win their first and only NBA title.

The defending champion Celtics hung in there all the way, with Russell playing twenty minutes with a heavily taped ankle. But every time the Hawks needed a basket down the stretch, Pettit came up with one. He put the Hawks in front to stay, 95–93. And all three times the Celtics closed to within a point, Pettit hit a shot to keep the Hawks on top. When it was over, Pettit had scored 19 points in the final quarter—in fact, he scored 19 of the Hawks' last 21 points.

To be sure, Pettit was not a one-man show. The 5′10″ guard Slater Martin held Bob Cousy to fifteen points and ran out the clock by dribbling the ball for the final nine seconds. But when the buzzer sounded and the St. Louis crowd of 10,218 stood and cheered, it was Pettit who was lifted onto his teammates' shoulders.

Had Russell been healthy, the entire series may have been different. But 1958 turned out to be the year of the Hawks, and there hasn't been another one since.

Russell and Chamberlain—Feud or Friendship?

During the 1960s, there was no better matchup in sports than the one between Bill Russell, playing for the Celtics, and Wilt Chamberlain, playing for the Warriors, 76ers, and then the Lakers. While Wilt was the one who would lead the NBA in scoring, setting records along the way, Russell was the one who would always seem to find a way to win.

Their head-to-head battles were classics, especially during the playoffs. Eight times their teams met in postseason play, and seven times Russell and the Celtics came out on top. The press frequently labeled Chamberlain a "loser." And basketball fans believed that the two great centers were mortal enemies.

In fact, however, Russell and Chamberlain were good friends during the entire length of their playing careers. They socialized together almost every time their teams played each other. And for several years in a row they shared Thanksgiving dinner at Wilt's house in Philadelphia, before the annual Turkey Day meeting between their two clubs.

Although Chamberlain resented the way he was portrayed in the press, he didn't let it harm their friendship. In 1967, Wilt's day finally arrived, as the 76ers ended the Celtics' string of eight straight championships. They routed the Celtics four games to one, winning the final game 140–116 as Chamberlain racked up the unbelievable combination of 29 points, 36 rebounds, and 13 assists.

The real friction between the two giants occurred after Russell had retired as a player, and stemmed from Russell's final game. In 1968–69, Russell was Boston's player-coach, and it would be his last year as a player. In the seventh game of the NBA finals, the Celtics were at Los Angeles against Chamberlain and the Lakers. With five minutes left and the Celtics leading by 13 points, Wilt took himself out of the game with a bruised shin. A few minutes later, the game

Russell vs. Chamberlain: battle of the giants

had become closer and Wilt wanted to return, but Laker Coach Bill van Breda Kolff would not put him back in the game. The Celtics held on to win by 2, but many observers believed the Lakers would have won if Wilt had stayed in the game.

Russell was angry at Wilt for leaving what would be Russell's final game, although Wilt did not know that Russell was going to retire. After retiring, Russell told an audience that if Chamberlain had to come out of that seventh game, he should have gone straight to a hospital. Russell went on to say that you can't quit like that and win championships.

It did not take long for the wire services to run a story saying that Russell had called Chamberlain a quitter. Reporters called Wilt, who responded with some derogatory remarks about Russell. Their friendship had taken a severe turn for the worse, but in the minds of most fans, it was merely a continuation of a long-running feud.

The First Olympic Basketball Tournament

Although American basketball teams had played exhibition games at the Olympics as far back as 1904, it was not until 1936 that basketball became an Olympic sport. The breakthrough came largely from the efforts of University of Kansas coach Phog Allen, who began campaigning for it in 1927. When the First International Basketball Conference was held in Geneva in 1932, it became obvious that basketball was truly an international game.

Basketball's Olympic debut took place in Berlin, with twenty-two countries entered in the tournament. As it turned out, only twenty-one of them took the court, as the team from Spain was recalled to its country when the Spanish Civil War broke out. In a fitting tribute to the inventor of basketball, Dr. James Naismith was flown to Berlin to watch the Olympics as an honored guest.

Some of the better teams from around the world were those representing Poland, the Philippines, and Uruguay. But most of the experts expected the North American teams to dominate, and they were correct.

The first Olympic basketball final was held on August 14, 1936, between the United States and Canada. The game was played on an outdoor court that was pelted with rain and became very muddy. High winds made the playing conditions even tougher.

The United States roared out to a 15–4 lead in the first half, and not much happened after that. The Americans held on to win 19–8. Joe Fortenberry, a 6′8″ center from McPherson, Kansas, took scoring honors with 8 points and stopped two Canadian shots by leaping up and catching the ball on its way to the basket.

The Americans were taller and more talented, and would probably have won by a larger margin had it not been for the weather conditions and a persistent zone defense employed by the Canadians. But they left little doubt as to where the worlds' best basketball was played.

North American basketball enjoyed another boost when Mexico defeated Poland 26–12 to win the bronze medal, giving this continent a sweep of the first Olympic medals.

In evaluating the impact of basketball's first Olympics, *The New York Times* put it best, stating, "The tournament proved two things. First, it is now clear that basketball no longer is merely an American game, but a genuine world game. The tournament proved, in the second place, however, that North America still is unthreatened in its basketball supremacy."

The NBA Scoring Champion Takes a Year Off

When Rick Barry broke into pro ball with the San Francisco Warriors in 1965, a lot of folks doubted that he would score the way he did at the University of Miami. The slender Barry was 6′7″ but only 200 pounds, and some questioned his ability to stand up to the physical pounding he would take as a pro.

Those doubts faded quickly as Barry averaged over 25 points a game and won the Rookie of the Year Award. The following year, he poured in over 35 points a game to win the NBA scoring championship. Barry and teammate Nate Thurmond led the Warriors to the NBA finals, where they were beaten by Wilt Chamberlain's 76ers. But Warrior fans expected big things from their team for years to come.

Unfortunately for them, the ABA was just getting started, with a team in Oakland that had its sights set on Rick Barry. The Oakland club was owned by singer and actor Pat Boone, who adroitly hired Bruce Hale to be his coach. Not only had Bruce Hale been Barry's college coach at Miami, but he was also Rick's father-in-law.

Warriors owner Franklin Mieuli made a serious bid to keep Barry, but on June 20, 1967, Rick became the first NBA star to jump to the new league. Barry signed a three-year contract with Oakland that was reported to be worth $500,000, although it was later revealed that his playing salary for the first year was closer to $75,000. As it turned out, Barry received that first year's salary for not playing.

When Rick signed with the Oakland Americans, the Warriors claimed that he had no right to do so, that his NBA contract from the previous season gave them the exclusive right to his services the following season. They promptly sought and received a court injunction preventing Barry from playing for anyone other than the Warriors.

The judge ruled that Barry was bound to the Warriors for one more year, but that if he sat out a season, he could then play for Oakland, although the Americans would have to pay damages to the Warriors for the loss of Barry's services. That was Barry's only alternative to playing for San Francisco.

It was an option he took to reluctantly but gamely. He prepared for his current profession by working for the Oakland team as a broadcaster. He also made personal appearances that boosted ticket sales around the ABA. A variety of endorsements and talent fees earned him over $100,000, but he was burning to return to the court.

When he did return the next year, he was back in top form, as he led the ABA in scoring with a 34-point average, and guided Oakland to the ABA championship. It was certainly agonizing for a league scoring champion to have to sit out a year in his prime, but in the end it was probably worth it for Rick Barry and the ABA. Barry went on to have a long, outstanding career, and the upstart league was a strong competitor for years to come.

Former NBA scoring champion Rick Barry

The Franklin Wonder Five

The state of Indiana is legendary for the quality of its schoolboy basketball teams and the fervor of the fans who follow them. In the long hardwood history of Hoosierland, no team has been as successful or caused the excitement created by the Franklin Wonder Five back in the 1920s.

Coached by a man named Griz Wagner, the high-school team from Franklin in south-central Indiana first gained notice in 1919. Sparked by fourteen-year-old freshman forward Robert "Fuzzy" Vandivier, Franklin went 18–2, but lost in the state tournament.

In 1920, they captured the state title, winning the championship game 31–13 to finish with a record of 29–1. But four of the five starters graduated that year, leaving only Vandivier to build the team around. Coach Wagner moved Fuzzy to center and surrounded him with four players who, although new as starters, were not exactly strangers. Many of them had played together as far back as grade school, practicing after school in a nearby barn.

The new Franklin team quickly clicked. They made it to the state finals again, played that year at the Indiana State Fairgrounds Coliseum. Over 10,000 fans, then the largest basketball crowd ever, watched Franklin repeat as state champions, 35–22.

When Franklin reached the finals again in 1922, a total of 12,000 fans packed the Coliseum. Back in Franklin, those fans who had not made the trip to Indianapolis crowded into the opera house, where the score was updated on an electric scoreboard.

Franklin again came out on top, 26–15, emptying the opera house for a huge celebration in the public square, complete with a gigantic bonfire. A few days later an official victory party and parade were held, featuring Izetta, touted as the "best woman accordion player in the world."

Nothing but the best for the team that had just become the first ever to win three straight Indiana state titles. To this day, they remain the only team ever to do so. But Coach Wagner's team was not finished winning.

In April, Griz Wagner left Franklin High School to become athletic director and basketball coach at Franklin College. A tough decision, undoubtedly, but it was made easier by a salary of $4,000 a year.

Wagner brought four of his high-school seniors along with him, including Fuzzy Vandivier. Starting a lineup consisting entirely of college freshmen, Franklin College won their first game, 69–7, and went on to win the state college championship. When they defeated highly rated Wabash, someone dubbed them the Wonder Five, and the name stuck.

The Wonder Five finished the year with a perfect 18–0 record. They even won a pair of games from one of the best professional teams in the country, the Omars, despite being at least five years younger and forty pounds lighter per man.

Now heralded by many as the best college team ever, their reputation was further enhanced the next year when they beat the Fighting Irish in South Bend during the Knute Rockne era. In summing up the game, a South Bend newspaper stated, "Franklin is to the hardwood court what Notre Dame is to the gridiron."

The Wonder Five was receiving national newspaper coverage and playing before packed houses wherever they went. Known for their great teamwork and sportsmanship, they won a second Indiana college title and ran their winning streak to 50 before finally losing to Butler.

The next year, the team failed to win their state title for the first time in six years, due partly to a rib injury suffered by Vandivier while fighting a fire in his fraternity house. Then, in his senior year, Vandivier missed much of the season with a spinal infection, and Wagner was unable to coach because of ulcers on both eyes that forced him to stay in darkened rooms. The team struggled in with a 13–6 record, and their dynasty was over.

But, in the state of Indiana, the legend of the Wonder Five lives on.

The Original Celtics

The Original Celtics

Originally organized as the New York Celtics in 1914, the Original Celtics were the world's most celebrated team in the 1920s. Promoter Jim Furey created basketball's first cohesive unit by signing the Celtics' players to exclusive contracts with guaranteed salaries. Never before had pro basketball players been tied to a single team, and Furey's move paid big dividends.

Billed as the "Original Celtics," the six players signed to those first contracts were all from New York City. Most were from tough neighborhoods, and they were a hard-nosed crew. Additions to the club in later years were just as rugged.

They started by playing every Sunday night at the same gym in New York, but soon began barnstorming up and down the East Coast and throughout the Midwest.

While on the road, the players became accustomed to roughing it, sometimes wearing the same uniforms for weeks without getting a chance to wash them. They had no real medical care, using home remedies to cure their ailments; they often had to pour brandy over open wounds. Not only were the Original Celtics tough, they were also shrewd, and they became the game's first great innovators.

In those days, there was a jump ball after every basket, and the Celtics invented the first tap play. Big Joe Lapchick would usually control the tap, and two passes later, the Celtics had an easy layup—often, several times in a row before the opposition could adjust.

Once, a team from Chattanooga tried to break up the Celtics' passing game by using a "standing guard," a player who remained at his own foul line and never went up court on offense. The Celtics figured out that they could neutralize the standing guard by stationing one of their own big men, Dutch Dehnert, right in front of him. The guards would pass the ball back and forth to Dehnert, and if the defender tried to intercept, Dehnert would have an easy layup. Celtic guard Nat Holman refined the play even further by teaching Dehnert to come forward to catch the passes to further protect the ball. This was the birth of the "pivot play," or post play, which remains a key part of most offenses today.

The Celtics also made a major contribution to defensive strategy. All teams in their era played a strict man-to-man defense, but the Celtics invented the "switch." Celtics defenders would switch the men they were guarding to help out a teammate who was out of position. This tactic rapidly became an integral part of basketball team defense.

During the 1920s, the Celtics played about 130 games a year, averaging 120 wins and 10 losses, so they had plenty of opportunity to perfect their new strategies. With a changing cast of characters, they continued barnstorming into the 1940s, but they never again attained the level of success of their early years.

While the Original Celtics eventually faded from the scene, their scientific approach to the game had an eternal impact on the basketball playbook.

The Birth of the NIT

In the mid-1930s, New York City was the mecca of college basketball. Sportswriter Ned Irish had become the sport's top promoter by packing Madison Square Garden for doubleheaders matching the top New York teams against schools from around the country. City College and NYU were the traditional New York powers, with keen competition from St. John's, Seton Hall, Long Island University, Fordham, and a host of others.

In 1938, the Metropolitan Basketball Writers Association sponsored the first postseason tournament—the National Invitational Tournament—for teams from different parts of the nation. As the name suggests, the writers invited the teams.

Six schools were invited to that first tournament, with Colorado and Oklahoma A&M receiving byes in the first round.

The two New York entries played each other in the first round, with NYU beating Long Island University. In the other first-round game, Temple knocked off Bradley. In the second round, Colorado beat NYU, but Temple upset seeded Oklahoma A&M. Then the Temple Owls shocked the other seeded team, Colorado, 60–36, to become the first NIT champion.

The tournament was a huge success, which prompted the NCAA to stage its own postseason tournament in 1939. Instead of stepping aside, however, the NIT put on an even bigger show that year and landed the country's two glamour teams.

In a matchup made in basketball heaven, the final game of the second NIT featured the nation's only two undefeated teams, the Blackbirds of Long Island University (LIU) and the Loyola of Chicago Ramblers. Under legendary coach Clair Bee, LIU had incredible depth, and used twelve different players in the final. The score: LIU 44, Loyola 32, as the Blackbirds finished their season with a record of 24–0.

In the first NCAA tournament that same year, Pacific Coast Conference champion Oregon met Western Conference champion Ohio State in the final, played at Northwestern University in Evanston, Illinois. The "Tall Firs" of Oregon triumphed 46–33.

When the next season began, the defending NIT and NCAA champions played each other in the first doubleheader at Madison Square Garden. Early in the second half, Oregon led LIU by 15 points. But the Blackbirds rallied to tie it up, and then won it in overtime.

The NIT champion was established as the nation's top team, a pattern that was to continue for a number of years. Eventually, of course, the NCAA tournament prevailed as the national championship competition while the NIT had to accept a lesser role. Finally, the NIT was moved to the start of the season, where it would no longer have to settle for the teams unwanted by the NCAA. For many years, though, the goal of every team was to make it to the NIT, the first inter-regional postseason college basketball tournament.

The Star the Pistons Didn't Want

For twelve years in the 1960s and '70s, Dave Bing was one of the premier guards in the NBA. Playing in the shadow of superstars Oscar Robertson and Jerry West, Bing averaged over 20 points a game in his career, including a league-leading 27 points a game in 1967–68. Twice he made the all-NBA first team ahead of either Robertson or West, despite playing for Detroit Piston teams that were far from championship caliber.

At 6′3″ and 180 pounds, Bing was smaller than most of the men he played against, but he used his incredible quickness to drive on anyone. And he usually ranked at the top of the league in assists as well as in scoring.

Born in a ghetto in Washington, DC, Dave realized early that a college

Standout guard
Dave Bing

scholarship was his best way out. In a tournament of high-school All-Americans, Bing was the Most Valuable Player, and the scholarship offers rolled in. UCLA offered one, as did Michigan and many other national powers. Some schools were offering money under the table, but Bing refused to take it, choosing instead to attend Syracuse, at the time not known for its basketball teams.

A humble young man, Bing was not sure he could stand out at a national power and figured he'd be better off as the big fish in a small pond. That he was, as he averaged close to 25 points a game in his three seasons at Syracuse and became an All-American.

When Bing left Syracuse in 1966, the Detroit Pistons were the worst team in the NBA and were badly in need of an explosive scorer. But Dave Bing was not the man they wanted. They coveted Cazzie Russell, who had starred at nearby University of Michigan and would have been an instant gate attraction. But first, the Pistons (who had finished last in the West) would have to win a coin flip with the New York Knicks (last in the East) to see who would get the number-one pick.

Fortunately for the Pistons, they lost the flip, and when the Knicks drafted Russell, Detroit settled for Bing. By then, Dave was confident that he could play with anyone, so he quickly moved his wife and children to Detroit. But the Piston fans were not entirely hospitable. In his first few home games at Cobo Arena, Bing was greeted with chants of "We want Cazzie!" But those cries didn't last long because Bing, undaunted, became an instant star.

Soon, Piston fans were screaming "Bingo" whenever Dave would hit a shot with a defender draped all over him. And, while Cazzie Russell was struggling in New York to adjust to pro ball, Bing walked away with the Rookie of the Year Award.

Russell went on to have a fine NBA career as a sixth man and played on one championship team. But he never achieved the individual stardom of the man the Pistons landed only through the good fortune of losing a coin flip—Dave Bing.

The Spectacularly Short Career of Ernie D

Never has a man broken into the NBA as brilliantly and gone out as quickly as six-foot ball-handling wizard Ernie DiGregorio. A product of his hometown school, Providence College, "Ernie D" decided by the time he was five that he wanted to play basketball for a living. Through hours and hours of practice at neighborhood playgrounds, his dream was realized.

Despite receiving letters from hundreds of colleges, Ernie never considered leaving home, where his heroes had been Providence stars Johnny Egan and Jimmy Walker. In three varsity years with the Friars, he averaged 20.5 points a game, but he was known more for his dazzling ball-handling and sensational passing.

As a senior in 1973, he led the Friars to a 27–2 record and a berth in the Final Four. In the first half of the semifinal game against Memphis State, Ernie put on an incredible display with 17 points and 7 assists, as he was responsible for 18 of his team's 22 baskets. One of those assists came on a behind-the-back-pass that he launched the length of the court, a full eighty feet in the air.

The Friars led at the half 49–40, but lost their big man, Marvin Barnes, to a knee injury in the second half. That cost them the game despite Ernie D's 32-point night. The Buffalo Braves soon made him their first-round draft and won a bidding war for his services from the ABA Kentucky Colonels. The ABA wanted Ernie badly, feeling he was the key to their landing a national television contract. Ernie intended all along to play in the NBA, but he allowed the price to escalate to a lofty $2 million for five years.

Ernie D was to be the NBA's highest-paid player, and announced his goal was to lead the league in assists and free throw percentage. Some skeptics scoffed, thinking him too small and too slow, but Ernie D proved them wrong. He led the league in both departments as a rookie and made a joke out of the Rookie of the Year voting, winning by a margin of 115–17 over runner-up Ron Behagen.

More important, Ernie led Buffalo to their first playoff berth, as they doubled their victory total. They also came close to knocking the Celtics out of the playoffs in a tough six-game series. Braves coach Jack Ramsey called Ernie "the best passer I've ever seen, with the possible exception of Bob Cousy."

Ernie's ballhandling tricks made him a favorite of fans around the league. A *Time* magazine article dubbed him "The Italian Leprechaun." At the start of his second year, Ernie was invited to the White House to a dinner honoring the president of Italy. But Ernie did have his critics.

DiGregorio was often maligned for his poor defensive play. Low-scoring Dean Meminger poured in 27 points against him, and when an injured Jerry West scored 35 points on him in thirty-two minutes, a Los Angeles writer dubbed DiGregorio "Ernie No D." Most observers conceded, however, that Ernie remained on the plus side of the ledger in points created compared with points allowed.

In his second season, Ernie suffered a knee injury that cost him most of the season. When he returned the next year, he was a step slower and was relegated to a backup role. Ernie sulked at the end of the bench and was often booed by the fans. He played more the next year, averaging about a half per game, but then was sold to the Lakers for virtually nothing with a year to go on his contract. Appearing in only 25 games in his final season, Ernie D never got another NBA contract.

That one knee injury and the coming of bigger, faster guards made the career of Ernie D a short-lived dream come true.

The First Great One-handed Shooter

Until the mid-1930s, basketball players were taught to shoot the ball with two hands, and very few players were willing to challenge their coaches and shoot with just one hand. Then suddenly, a glamorous fellow named Angelo "Hank" Luisetti rode in from the West and revolutionized the game forever.

Luisetti was the 6′3″ star who turned Stanford into a national power and introduced the one-hand push shot to the college basketball teams of the East. Born in the same San Francisco neighborhood that produced Joe DiMaggio, Luisetti began playing basketball at the age of six, but it was not until high school that he began fooling around with the one-handed shot. He was so accurate that his coach allowed him to shoot in this unorthodox fashion, and at Stanford, he perfected the technique.

His freshman team at Stanford went undefeated in 1934–35, and as a sophomore, Hank led the varsity to the Pacific Coast Conference title. Basketball fans in the East were beginning to hear about the handsome, black-haired sensation with the one-hand shot, but most of the easterners remained skeptical about a westerner being able to teach them anything about their game of basketball. That all changed the following year.

In December of 1936, Hank Luisetti came east with his one-handed shot and his Stanford teammates, and the game of basketball has not been the same since. First, they knocked off a strong Temple team 45–38, with Luisetti leading the way. Then they had a chance to play what everyone thought was the nation's best team, Long Island University, winner of 43 consecutive games.

Most easterners continued to believe in the philosophy preached by City College coach Nat Holman (one of the Original Celtics), who said, "I'll quit coaching if I have to teach one-handed shots to win. There's only one way to shoot, and that's the way we do it in the East—with two hands."

A crowd of 17,623 jammed into Madison Square Garden for their first look at the one-handed wonder. They came away believing that Hank had the right idea. His Stanford team crushed Long Island 45–31, with Luisetti scoring 15 points and dominating the game with his dribbling, passing, and rebounding as well. As he left the court, Luisetti received a standing ovation from a Garden crowd that had been totally captivated by his performance.

As *The New York Times* reported the next day, "It seemed Luisetti could do nothing wrong. Some of his shots would have been deemed foolhardy if attempted by anybody else, but with Luisetti shooting, these were accepted by the crowd as a matter of course."

Actually, Luisetti did not invent the one-hand shot. But he was the first to use it accurately in front of large crowds. He could shoot one-handed from all positions, while running as well as when set. He could even shoot while in the air, thus pioneering the jump shot as well. It didn't take long for kids around the country to imitate Luisetti, who became an instant national hero.

He was college basketball's first superstar, a matinee idol who changed the game . . . singlehandedly. He was the country's Player of the Year twice in a row, and led Stanford to three straight Pacific Coast Conference titles. In 1936–37, the year they snapped Long Island University's 43-game winning streak, Luisetti's Stanford team was voted collegiate team of the year.

While Luisetti was the game's biggest star, he was also a very well rounded

Stanford star Hank Luisetti

and unselfish player. In fact, his teammates felt he passed the ball too much and didn't take enough shots. One night in 1938 they decided to force him to shoot. Playing against a strong Duquesne team on a neutral court in Cleveland, they decided that to get Luisetti to shoot more, they would return all his passes right back to him.

The result was a 50-point explosion by Luisetti as the Indians ripped the Dukes 92–27. When the season was over, Luisetti had ended his college career with a total of almost 1,600 points, a new collegiate record that averaged out to 16.5 points per game.

Hank Luisetti was a national hero, envisioning a brilliant future. But his next career move turned out to be a big mistake. Because of Hank's classic good looks, many in Hollywood saw Luisetti as a potential box-office star. When he left Stanford in 1938, he received $10,000 to appear in a movie about basketball entitled *Campus Confessions*. Although the film starred the popular Betty Grable, it was a flop, and a serious blow to Luisetti's career in more ways than one.

The Amateur Athletic Union suspended him for a year, ruling that in making the movie, he had acted as a professional, and had lost his amateur status. The suspension kept Luisetti out of basketball's featured event, the national tournament, until 1940, when he returned to set a tournament scoring record. But his career was interrupted again, this time by World War II.

Luisetti enlisted in the navy and played a lot of basketball in the service. But in 1944 he came down with spinal meningitis. Although he recovered, the doctors told him that he would be risking his health if he played basketball again.

Having lost his chance at a lucrative pro career, Luisetti went into coaching for a while, and his team won the AAU championship in 1951. We can only wonder how big an impact he could have had on the professional game if an unfortunate series of circumstances had not denied college basketball's first superstar a chance to play pro ball.

How Many Players Did You Say?

When James Naismith invented basketball in 1891, he felt that the size of the teams could vary tremendously. But it wasn't long before a couple of games carried this idea to ridiculous extremes.

Naismith's original rules state that the number of players on each team "depends largely on the size of the floor space, but it may range from three on a side to forty. The fewer players down to three, the more scientific it may be made, but the more players, the more fun."

Word of the new game spread rapidly, thanks in part to the missionarylike efforts of the first players, and also because of an article in *The New York Times* in 1892. The *Times* referred to the new game as "a substitute for football without its rough features."

That same year, the new game spread to Cornell University in Ithaca, New York. Physical Education director Ed Hitchcock had one hundred students in his gym class, and he decided to stretch Naismith's guidelines a bit. He simply divided his class into two teams of fifty and let them go at it. The mayhem that followed threatened to bust up the Cornell gymnasium, and it quickly became obvious that fifty on a team was far too many.

Because so many people wanted to play, there was not very much of the other extreme envisioned by Naismith, the three-man team. But in one important game, a three-man team took the court by accident.

In 1897, the basketball rules were officially changed, setting the number of players on the court at five per team. But the first great team, the Buffalo Germans, had to take the court with only three players for a crucial game in 1901. It was the seventh and final game of the Pan-American Exposition, which was played in the Germans' hometown of Buffalo, New York. Three of the Germans were late for the game against St. Joseph's of Paterson, New Jersey, leaving the team with only three players as the game began.

The Germans' three-man team did a masterful job in holding off St. Joseph's in the early going, and the game was tied 1–1 after seven minutes when reinforcements began to arrive. First one player showed up on a bicycle, having pedaled frantically to get there before it was too late. A fifth man arrived a couple of minutes later, but with no time to change into his uniform, he had to play in his street clothes until the halftime break.

Once the Germans reached full strength, the game was no contest, as they blew away the opposition 10–1 to win the tournament. Perhaps they could have won even if the last two players had not shown up. But that's hardly what James Naismith had in mind when he thought the game could be played by three-man teams.

Chamberlain Retires After Rookie Pro Season

Wilt Chamberlain's arrival in the NBA in 1959 had been anticipated as far back as his sophomore year in high school in Philadelphia. During his three years at the University of Kansas, he grew to a height of 7′1″ and further enhanced his reputation as a sure-fire pro superstar. Instead of playing his senior year at Kansas, he joined the Harlem Globetrotters for a year, where he improved his ballhandling as well as his shooting.

There was never any doubt who Wilt would play for in the NBA. Philadelphia Warriors owner Eddie Gottlieb had convinced the league to expand the scope of their "territorial draft pick," which teams could use to draft college players from their area. In Chamberlain's case, Gottlieb had this rule extended to the player's high school, as the Warriors successfully drafted the coveted giant.

Gottlieb's idea was to have Chamberlain play as much as possible and score at every opportunity. After all, he was paying Wilt a reported $65,000, the highest salary in NBA history, and scoring records would pay off at the box office.

No one could say that Wilt failed to do exactly what was asked of him. In his first season as a pro, he set an NBA record by averaging 37.6 points a game. He played over forty-six minutes a game and led the league in rebounding. And not only did he win the Rookie of the Year Award, he won the MVP Award as well.

Wilt's heroics led the Warriors to a second-place finish in the East with a record of 49–26. But they lost to the Celtics in the second round of the playoffs.

Chamberlain was not happy. Throughout the entire season he had taken a terrible beating as opponents tried to keep him away from the basket. Opposing centers quickly realized that the best way to contain Wilt was to foul him. Since he was a poor free throw shooter, hitting only 58% from the line, he was deliberately fouled, and fouled hard.

In one game, Wilt was trying to move Hawks center Clyde Lovellette away from the basket. At 6′8″ and 235 pounds, Lovellette was giving away fifty pounds in the matchup with Chamberlain, and responded with a vicious elbow that broke four of Chamberlain's front teeth.

This incident and the long season of physical abuse took their toll on Chamberlain. Immediately after the Warriors' final playoff game against the Celtics, Wilt announced that he had had enough, and was retiring. Though he had broken the league's scoring record and proved his worth by having the greatest individual season the NBA had ever seen, he felt the game was too violent and unrewarding. He wanted to be a successful businessman, appreciated for his intelligence.

Not many people took Wilt's retirement seriously. Fortunately, he changed his mind in time for the next season: Wilt Chamberlain's long, record-breaking career had barely begun.

Wilt Chamberlain

A Giant Disappointment

Walter Dukes was one of the first seven-footers to play the game with grace and agility and was one of the greatest college players ever. A two-time All-American, Dukes led Seton Hall to a major college record of 27 straight wins in 1953. That same year, he set an NCAA record for rebounds in a season, averaging over 22 a game. He was the first player ever to average 20 points and 20 rebounds in his college career, and he's still one of just a handful who have accomplished that feat.

Dukes was quick and had very good reflexes, unlike most of the big men of his day. He was a good shooter, too, and had the moves to fake his opponent out of position. He was so unique that when the Knicks made him the first pick in the 1953 draft, they had to contend with a big offer that Dukes had received from the Harlem Globetrotters. When the Knicks would not match the Globetrotters' $17,000 bonus, they lost him. Dukes spent two years with the Globetrotters, and many feel that in doing so he acquired some bad habits that hurt him when he eventually joined the Knicks in 1955.

Dukes was a disappointment as an NBA rookie. He was guilty of repeated turnovers, especially traveling violations. He committed too many fouls and was a disciplinary problem, often late for workouts. He averaged only 8 points and 7 rebounds over the entire season. The next year, he was suspended in training camp. Knicks coach Vince Boryla said, "He's not the type of player we want. He doesn't have the temperament, the spirit, or the attitude." Two weeks later, Dukes was no longer a Knick.

In a bizarre trade involving the NBA's tallest and shortest players, Dukes was shipped to the Lakers for 5′10″ guard Slater Martin. A year later, the Lakers traded him to the Pistons. While his career didn't exactly skyrocket, Dukes went on to set two NBA records with the Pistons.

At 7′0″ and 220 pounds, Walter was considered the NBA's roughest and most painful player to go up against. He was a terror under the boards, especially on the offensive end of the floor. Known for having "the sharpest elbows in the NBA," Dukes was among the league's top 8 rebounders in each of his first four seasons with the Pistons. But in each of those years, he also led the NBA in fouling out of games.

Leading the league in disqualifications four times remains an NBA record. Even more unusual is the fact that it was set in consecutive years. While Dukes played two more seasons without leading the league, he retired with another NBA record that may never be broken. In 553 NBA games, Dukes fouled out of 121, a record percentage of 21.88, or better than one out of every five games. No one in NBA history has even come close to approaching that percentage of disqualifications.

Not even Walter's teammates were safe from his thrashing elbows. In fact, Piston teammate Bailey Howell claimed, "Walter hurts me worse than anybody else." One day in practice, the Pistons tied a bell around Walter's neck so they would know where he was and could avoid his uncontrollably swinging arms.

A very different person off the court, Dukes was intelligent, well-read, and an accomplished pilot who composed classical music in his spare time. He graduated from law school while playing pro basketball, and attained financial success in real estate and travel agencies. He even made strides toward being more prompt, an attempt that cost him in 1959.

Walter had held out that year for three weeks before signing, and wanted to be sure he would leave for Detroit on time the next day. So he packed his car late at night, only to find when he awoke that his car had been broken into and his clothing stolen.

Who could wear the suits and shirts belonging to a seven-footer? Who knows—but whoever stole them only added to the legend of Walter Dukes, a true one-of-a-kind.

Maurice Stokes' career ended all too quickly.

The Tragic Story of Maurice Stokes

Until the mid-1950s, most basketball fans had never heard of St. Francis College in Loretto, Pennsylvania. But they learned about it quickly when Maurice Stokes came along. A 6′7″ center who was strong and muscular, Stokes was also extremely agile. He could shoot, rebound, and play defense, and he did it all with a remarkable smoothness for a man of his size.

After a brilliant college career at St. Francis, Stokes was picked by the Rochester Royals in the first round of the 1955 NBA draft. "Big Mo" rapidly proved himself to be the cream of the league's rookie crop, finishing second in the league in rebounds with 16 a game and averaging 17 points. He was an easy choice for the Rookie of the Year Award and followed up that honor by leading the league in rebounds in his second season.

The next year the Royals moved to Cincinnati, and Stokes helped lead the team into the playoffs with 18 rebounds and 17 points a game. That was to be his final year in basketball. In the last regular-season game, Stokes tripped and fell, hitting his head on the floor, and was knocked out cold for three minutes before being revived.

A few days later, Stokes played against the Pistons in a playoff game at Detroit, but he was obviously off his game and complained of headaches. On the flight back to Cincinnati he became violently ill and lapsed into a coma. Doctors determined Stokes had encephalitis, which caused brain damage that left him paralyzed. They predicted he would never be able to move or talk again.

Stokes was in dire need of support, both personal and financial, and Royal teammate Jack Twyman quickly went into action to help. Twyman had himself named as Stokes' legal guardian and raised money to pay his hospital bills. He convinced the league to stage a benefit game to raise money for its fallen star; just six months later, the first Maurice Stokes Benefit Game raised over $10,000.

Twyman also provided the friendship that Stokes needed. He visited him often and they worked out a system in which Stokes could communicate by blinking his eyes. Eventually, Maurice surprised the doctors by learning to speak again. Through exhausting physical therapy, he regained some of the movement in his hands.

In 1967 Stokes was flown to New York to attend his own benefit game. He received an overwhelming ovation from fans and players when he was wheeled onto the court. His battle to survive was a courageous one, but the struggle was finally lost when Stokes died in 1970.

The loss of Maurice Stokes was horribly tragic, but the character exemplified by Stokes, and the loyalty shown by his friend Jack Twyman, has been an inspiration that shows no sign of fading.

The ABL Breaks up the Celtics

A cry of "Break up the Celtics!" was often heard during the Boston dynasty years of the 1960s. While it was then said facetiously, that same plan had actually been carried out by the American Basketball League over thirty years earlier.

Formed in 1925, the ABL was the first pro basketball league to go beyond regional status, as it included teams from Boston all the way to Chicago. Teams signed their players to contracts that paid as much as $1,500 a month. Among the team owners were Washington's George Preston Marshall (who became best known as the long-time owner of the NFL Washington Redskins) and George Halas of the Chicago Bears.

Unfortunately for the new league, the best team in the land, the Original Celtics, refused to join, figuring that they would make more money by remaining independent. The Celtics did, though, play exhibitions against ABL teams, and typically crushed them with ease.

The Celtics presented a major problem to the league in its first year, but Marshall and the other owners finally came up with a solution. They decided to blacklist the Celtics, banning games between them and any ABL team. This left the Celtics without any really good teams to play, and without a chance to draw big crowds. They reluctantly joined the league for its second season in 1926.

Not surprisingly, the Celtics rolled through the league by winning 19 of 20 games in the second half of the season, and swept Cleveland in the playoffs to win the championship. The next year, they went 40–9 and won the title again. Cries of "Break up the Celtics!" were heard from fans around the league, and the owners took those pleas seriously.

The Celtics were so much better than the other teams in the ABL that fans were losing interest in the league and attendance was dropping rapidly. The troubled team owners heeded the fans' cries and finally disbanded the league's best team, dispersing the Celtic players to other clubs.

The Cleveland Rosenblums landed three of them, Joe Lapchick, Dutch Dehnert, and Pete Barry, and quickly became the class of the league. Referred to by some as the Rosenblum-Celtics, Cleveland won the next two ABL titles. But they never got a chance to win a third.

With the nation in the grip of the Great Depression, attendance became insufficient to cover player salaries, and in December of 1930, Cleveland owner Max Rosenblum folded his team. Although the league finished the season, it soon faded away. Although it was re-formed a few years later, it became strictly a regional circuit in the Northeast.

The idea of a national pro basketball league had been slightly ahead of its time. Not even breaking up the Original Celtics could make it succeed with such dire economic conditions working against it.

Basketball's All-time Best Collegian?

The debate over who was the greatest college basketball player of all time will never be resolved. But despite the heroics of stars like George Mikan, Bill Russell, Lew Alcindor, Bill Walton, and Larry Bird, it's tough to vote against "the Big O"—Oscar Robertson of the University of Cincinnati.

As a high-school star in Indianapolis, the Big O led his team to 45 straight wins and two state championships. All his life he had wanted to attend Indiana University. But Oscar's older brother Bailey, one of the best players in the state, was turned down by Indiana. Oscar felt Indiana had rejected Bailey because they had already admitted one black player that year, and the Big O decided that he would go elsewhere.

Indiana's loss became Cincinnati's gain. The school had never recruited a black player, and had never been highly ranked, but it landed the Big O. Coach George Smith of the Bearcats then watched as Robertson turned his team into a national power.

Robertson's impact was immediate. In 1958, his first varsity season, Robertson was named Player of the Year in college basketball. He led the country in scoring with over 35 points a game, easily outdistancing Elgin Baylor and Wilt Chamberlain. The Bearcats won their first Missouri Valley Conference title and finished with a 25–3 record, but they lost in the Midwest Regionals of the NCAA tournament.

All-American and NBA All-Star Oscar Robertson

The next year, as a junior, Robertson led the country in scoring again. Cincinnati went 26–4 and again won the conference title. This time they made it to the Final Four, only to lose in the semifinals to eventual national champion California.

Then, as a senior, the Big O made it three national scoring titles in a row, and three straight conference titles, as Cincinnati went 28–2. But for the second consecutive year, they lost in the NCAA semifinals to California, as the Golden Bears held Robertson to just 18 points.

So Robertson's teams never won an NCAA title. But his credentials as college basketball's all-time best player remain impeccable.

During his three varsity seasons, Oscar set an NCAA career scoring record, averaging 33.8 points a game. In one game at Madison Square Garden, Cincinnati routed Seton Hall 118–54; the Big O outscored Seton Hall by himself with 56 points. Lest you think that maybe Oscar was shooting too much, keep in mind that he also established an NCAA career record for assists, averaging 7 a game, and set twelve other NCAA records.

His Cincinnati teams were 79–9 and did not lose a single game at home. They were never lower than fifth in the national rankings. And although Oscar's teams never won a national championship, Robertson's successes allowed Cincinnati to recruit a team that won the national title each of the next two

Back-to-back Titles Without "The Big O"

Oscar Robertson was the nation's top player and Cincinnati was considered the best team in 1959 and 1960, but in both years, the Bearcats lost in the NCAA semifinals to California. With Robertson gone in 1961, not many people gave the Bearcats a chance to go all the way. The consensus favorite was their cross-state rival Ohio State, who had beaten California for the national championship in 1960, and who had returning stars Jerry Lucas, John Havlicek, and Larry Siegfried.

Ohio State's Buckeyes rolled through the 1960–61 season undefeated as one of the highest-scoring teams in college history. But Cincinnati, led by their strong frontcourt of Paul Hogue, Tom Thacker, and Bob Wiesenhahn, ran up a record of 27–3. The Bearcats had adjusted their game to a slower ball-control offense with a rugged defense, and this combination landed them in the NCAA finals against Ohio State.

The Buckeyes had a 34-game winning streak and were heavily favored. But Cincinnati played a nearly flawless game. Their defense held the Buckeyes to a mere 50 shots, and on offense they committed only 3 turnovers all night. Late in the game, Cincinnati led by 2 points, but the Buckeyes tied it with fifty-six seconds left on a driving layup by Bobby Knight. (Yes, it was that Bobby Knight, and it was his only basket of the game.)

The teams went into overtime at 61–61. Then Cincinnati took over, outscoring Ohio State 9–4 in the extra session to win the game and the national title, 70–65. Lucas scored 27 points in a losing cause, but he and his teammates would get another shot at the Bearcats the following year.

In 1962, defending champion Cincinnati again met Ohio State in the NCAA finals, and again the Buckeyes were ranked number one. Each team had lost a couple of players to graduation, but Hogue and Thacker were back for Cincinnati, Ohio State still had Lucas and Havlicek, and each team had three returning starters.

Cincinnati was out to prove that 1961 had been no fluke, and they repeated the defensive performance that had helped them win the championship game. Lucas was hobbled by an injured knee suffered in the semifinals, and Hogue took advantage by piling up a game-high 22 points and 19 rebounds. Lucas managed only 11 points, and the Buckeyes were taken out of the game early. Cincinnati built up an 8-point lead at halftime, and they were never threatened after that. The final score: Cincinnati 71, Ohio State 59.

Cincinnati's back-to-back victories over Ohio State were the only time that teams from the same state have played each other in consecutive NCAA finals. Surprisingly, the team that had lost its big star, Oscar Robertson, beat the team with the big-name players who had already won them a national title.

Picked Out of a Hat

In 1950, Bob Cousy wanted nothing more than to play for the Boston Celtics. He seemed to have a strong claim to a spot on their roster. An All-American guard at nearby Holy Cross in Worcester, Massachusetts, Cousy was a crowd pleaser who was already loved by the fans in Boston. He had played for a national championship team as a freshman, averaged almost 20 points a game as a senior, and was a ballhandler without equal. Surely, he was the man who could bring success to the losing Celtics, both on the court and at the box office.

Although that's how it appeared to the Boston fans and press, Celtics coach Red Auerbach had other ideas. Auerbach said that the 6′1″ Cousy was too small for the pro game and too flashy for the Celtics' style of play. He went so far as to refer to Cousy as a "local yokel." Thinking the Celtics needed a big man, Auerbach drafted 6′11″ Chuck Share of Bowling Green, while Cousy was picked in the first round by the Tri-Cities Hawks, who played in Moline and Rock Island, Illinois, and Davenport, Iowa.

Before Cousy played his first NBA game, he was traded to the Chicago Stags, a team that was going broke, so that Tri-Cities could acquire Chicago star Frankie Brian. When the Stags folded before the season started, their players were up for grabs, including Cousy and two outstanding NBA players, high-scoring Max Zaslofsky and playmaker Andy Phillip. Three teams were to choose among the three players: Boston, New York, and Philadelphia. Zaslofsky the scorer was the first choice of all three clubs.

On October 5, 1950, the NBA owners remained deadlocked over who should get Zaslofsky, until Syracuse owner Danny Biasone offered his hat for a drawing. Commissioner Max Podoloff placed three numbers in the hat. The Knicks plucked out number one and selected Zaslofsky. Philadelphia got number two and picked Andy Phillip. That left Boston owner Walter Brown "stuck" with Bob Cousy.

Without playing a single game, Cousy was now with his third pro team—and finally, the one he was meant to play for all along. He toned down his fancy dribbling and behind-the-back passing to adapt to the Celtics style, and he eventually became the playmaker for the Celtics' first six championship teams.

Cousy was a first-team All-Star ten years in a row, and he led the league in assists seven straight seasons. When he retired in 1963 after thirteen years in Boston, the Celtics put on a forty-three-minute pregame ceremony that was called "the most emotional sporting event in Boston history." It would never have happened if the wrong number had come out of a hat back in 1950.

Bob Cousy, more than a local yokel

The Man Who Scored Over 100 Points—Twice

Chances are, you've never heard of a man named Bevo Francis, or a school in Ohio called Rio Grande College. But back in the early 1950s, Francis and his school became synonymous with college basketball scoring records.

When Clarence "Bevo" Francis enrolled at Rio Grande in Jackson, Ohio, in 1952, the school had only ninety-four full-time students. Francis, who already had a wife and a son, was admitted to the school despite the lack of a high-school diploma. Basketball coach Newt Oliver somehow got Bevo admitted, after watching the way the 6′9″ Francis could shoot a basketball.

Coach Oliver was rewarded when Francis, in his freshman year, led the team to 39 wins in a row. Bevo averaged over 50 points a game, and in one game against Ashland Junior College he scored 116 points. But the NCAA refused to recognize Bevo's scoring records because so many of his opponents had been junior colleges and seminary and military service teams. And, in the NAIA tournament that year, Rio Grande was quickly eliminated.

The following year, Rio Grande's schedule was upgraded, and in mid-January, Francis set a small-college record that was recognized, an 84-point performance against Alliance College. Then, on February 2, 1954, Bevo bettered that mark.

In a home game against Hillsdale College of Michigan, Francis scored 43 points in the first half. Despite being guarded by three men, he finished the third quarter with 74. In the fourth quarter, Bevo poured in 39 points, for a one-game record of 113 points that will probably never be broken.

Francis hit about 75% of his shots that night, with most of them coming from a low-post position. Even fans in the Big Apple were captivated by Bevo's records, and wanted a chance to see him. Soon after his 113-point game, Francis and his Rio Grande teammates appeared at Madison Square Garden against Adelphi. Bevo scored 32 points in the first half, but was shut out completely in the second half as Adelphi used four men to cover him. With Bevo's teammates unable to sink their shots, Rio Grande lost 83–76.

Rio Grande then played Villanova and lost in a squeaker, with Bevo getting 39 points. Finally, they beat a major opponent, as Bevo scored 41 in a win over Providence College.

Francis finished that season with an average of 46.5 points a game, and made second-team All-American. Suddenly, he was expelled from school for missing classes and failing to take make-up exams. Coach Newt Oliver stated that if Bevo left, so would he. Together, Oliver and Francis signed with a minor pro team, the Boston Whirlwinds. But Francis was largely unsuccessful as a pro and never made it to the NBA.

Rio Grande College has faded into obscurity along with the name of Bevo Francis, but you'll still find both names big and bold in the college basketball record book.

Lew Alcindor with John Wooden

The Night Alcindor Ended UCLA's String of Titles

At UCLA, Lew Alcindor (now Kareem Abdul-Jabbar) is best remembered for leading the Bruins to three straight national championships. But how about the night he ruined the Bruins' chances of continuing a string of national titles?

UCLA's domination of college basketball began before Alcindor arrived in Los Angeles in 1965. For years, coach John Wooden had been hoping to put together the personnel capable of playing a full-court zone press, and in 1964 he finally had the right combination. Led by starting guards Gail Goodrich and Walt Hazzard and all-purpose substitute Kenny Washington, the Bruins rolled to an undefeated season. In the NCAA final they outscored Duke 98–83, establishing a new record for points in the championship game.

UCLA was only the third team ever to go all the way with a perfect record. And they did it without a single regular player taller than 6′5″. The next year, with Hazzard having graduated, their streak ended quickly. In their very first game, the Bruins were crushed by Illinois 110–83. But that was to be one of only two UCLA defeats all season. Goodrich became a bigger part of the offense, and in the NCAA final against Michigan, he scored 42 points as the Bruins beat the

Wolverines and Cazzie Russell 91–80.

The following year, Goodrich was gone, replaced by former Indiana high-school star Mike Warren. Most of the other regulars were back, and many people thought the Bruins had a great shot at a record-breaking third straight NCAA title. But before the 1965–66 season even started, they received a blow from which they never recovered.

On a night billed as Salute to John Wooden Night, a preseason exhibition game was held to officially open Pauley Pavilion. The place was packed, and a large local television audience tuned in to watch the two-time national champions oppose the best group of freshmen ever recruited by UCLA. Coached by Gary Cunningham, the freshman team started Lucius Allen from Kansas, Kent Taylor from Texas, Californians Kenny Heitz and Lynn Shackelford, and Alcindor.

They should have called it Salute to Lew Alcindor Night, as the seven-foot freshman from New York totally controlled the game. The freshmen humiliated the varsity 75–60, and would have won by more had they not cleared their bench late in the game.

Wooden had decided not to employ a special defense against Alcindor, so as not to alienate his future star, and the big man had a field day. Lew scored 31 points, pulled down 21 rebounds, blocked several shots, and even broke the zone press by handling the inbounds pass.

Alcindor and his mates dealt the varsity a psychological blow from which it never recovered. The defending national champions posted a disappointing 18–8 record, finishing second in their conference. And while Texas Western was winning the NCAA title, Bruin fans were gloating over their undefeated freshman team, which had gone 21–0 as Alcindor averaged 33 points and 21 rebounds.

But the one freshman win not included in that record was the one that may have ruined any chance of UCLA continuing their string of NCAA titles. Of course, a new streak would begin the following year—one unprecedented in the history of college basketball.

The Rule Changes That Saved the NBA

In the early years of the NBA, the pro game was troubled by two forms of stalling that slowed down the tempo and severely dampened spectator interest. The first was the strategy of sitting on a lead and refusing to shoot, so-called freezing the ball. But just as frustrating to the fan was the trailing team's tactic of deliberately fouling as soon as the opposition got the ball, hoping to trade one point on a free throw for a chance to score two points at the other end.

The tactics resulted in tedious games that seemed to last forever, with a seemingly interminable succession of whistles. Things got so bad that in one playoff game between Boston and Syracuse in March 1953 a total of 107 fouls were called in a game that lasted four overtime periods. While Bob Cousy of the Celtics set a playoff record by scoring 50 points, 30 of them came from the free throw line—hardly the most exciting scoring display you could imagine.

All this took place despite the limit of six fouls per player. In fact, seven Syracuse players had six fouls, but two of them had to stay in the game with a technical foul added anytime they committed another foul.

In the 1953–54 season, a new rule limited each player to two fouls per quarter, after which he would have to sit out the rest of that quarter. But the rule was ineffective, and the average team score dropped to 79.5 points a game. Clearly, the league needed a way to penalize a team, not just an individual, for excessive fouling. They also needed to outlaw the freeze.

On April 22, 1954, the NBA owners met with a willingness to find a solution, even a radical one, to the game's problems. The answer came from Syracuse owner Danny Biasone, who proposed the 24-second shot clock. Biasone had figured out that the league was averaging about one shot every eighteen seconds, and decided that twenty-four seconds would be a reasonable limit. The new rule was adopted, and the freezing problem had been solved.

Next, the league adopted a limit on team fouls, with only six permitted each quarter. After that, every foul would cost an extra free throw, including three chances to make two points if the player fouled was in the act of shooting. Another new rule made all backcourt fouls into two-shot fouls.

The new rules were tremendously successful. The shot clock made it unnecessary for the trailing team to foul to get the ball back, and the team foul limit all but eliminated the abuse of deliberate fouling.

The game became more wide open and free flowing, and much faster. The team scoring average jumped to 93.1 points a game, and the number of fouls dropped to less than fifty a game for both teams. The reigning dynasty of the Minneapolis Lakers was badly hurt by the new rules and some other clubs were helped, as basketball changed from a slow-it-down-and-set-it-up game to the fast-breaking, quick-shooting sport that we're familiar with today.

The Hawk's Lost Years

Born in 1942 in the Brooklyn, New York ghetto of Bedford-Stuyvesant, Connie Hawkins had the cards stacked against him. There were six kids in his family, and by the time he was ten, his father was gone and his mother was almost blind. Connie earned his self-respect on the playground basketball courts, and by the time he got to high school he was revered as the best schoolyard player in all of New York City.

Hawkins led his Boys High School team to two city championships and was the Most Valuable Player in the 1960 High-School All-Star Game featuring seniors from around the country. Despite a poor academic record, "the Hawk" received scholarship offers from over 250 colleges and decided to attend the University of Iowa. But he was soon called back to New York for questioning during a college basketball betting scandal.

While Connie was in high school, a former basketball star named Jack Molinas had befriended Hawkins, turning up wherever Connie was playing. Molinas frequently treated Hawkins to dinner and once loaned him $200, which Hawkins paid back. This association with Molinas ultimately cost Hawkins a chance to be one of basketball's all-time greats.

In the college basketball betting scandal of 1961, Molinas was convicted and sentenced to four years in a federal prison. Certainly, Hawkins had not been bribed by Molinas to fix games. That would have been impossible since he was only a college freshman and not yet eligible for varsity competition. But Hawkins admitted having spent time with Molinas, and he was thought to be guilty of associating with gamblers and introducing another player to gamblers. Iowa quickly canceled his scholarship, and no other schools would touch him. The NBA also declared Hawkins to be off-limits to its teams.

The 6′8″ Hawkins opted to play in the old American Basketball League and won its Most Valuable Player Award, but the league folded the next year. He joined the Harlem Globetrotters and spent four years with them before the ABA was born in 1967. Hawkins had two great years in the ABA including an MVP season. But he was determined to establish his innocence of the old charges and to play against the world's best players in the NBA.

A lawsuit finally helped get Connie Hawkins into the NBA.

Hawkins filed a $6 million lawsuit against the NBA, which helped persuade the league to change its policy. Connie was then allowed to sign an NBA contract with the Phoenix Suns that would earn him more than a million dollars over the next few years. He decided to drop his lawsuit. Finally, at the age of twenty-eight, he could concentrate entirely on basketball. Hawkins proceeded to average over 20 points a game in each of his first three NBA seasons.

Connie Hawkins played a total of seven years in the NBA before retiring at the age of thirty-four. He had a flamboyant crowd-pleasing style of offensive basketball that was a treat to behold. It's a shame that NBA fans were denied his first seven years as a pro.

The Year They Boycotted the Olympics

In this country 1968 was a year of unrest. College athletes of all races were upset with the way minorities were treated, and many decided to protest by boycotting the US Olympic Team. Some were protesting the participation of a team from South Africa, while others focused their dissent on what they felt was the racist nature of American society.

US Olympic coach Hank Iba conducted tryouts in the notable absence of college basketball's superstars—Lew Alcindor (now Kareem Abdul-Jabbar), Wes Unseld, Elvin Hayes, Bob Lanier, and Donnie May. The team selected by Iba had only a couple of "name" college players—Jo Jo White of Kansas and Charlie Scott of North Carolina. With all the great college big men joining in the boycott, the American team was considered unlikely to win anything more than a bronze medal at Mexico City.

The United States had won six Olympic basketball gold medals in a row, but now they were underdogs to a Russian team, which featured a 7′3″ center, and a team from Yugoslavia led by their high-scoring center Dragutin Cermak. Iba trained his team hard, and those unknowns made the most of the opportunity afforded them by the boycott. The brightest of the unknown stars, a nineteen-year-old named Spencer Haywood, became a national hero.

Before the 1968 Olympics, even the most ardent basketball fans were unaware of Haywood, unless they happened to see the 6′8″ center playing for Trinidad State Junior College in Colorado. They might also have seen him during a brilliant high-school career in Detroit.

When the Olympics began, Haywood and Jo Jo White quickly established that the American team was not without leadership. White ran the offense from his guard position while Haywood dominated the boards, as the Americans rolled over Spain, the Philippines, highly touted Yugoslavia, and Italy. Then they got a scare from Puerto Rico before winning 61–56, as Haywood scored twenty-one points. They beat Brazil to earn a spot in the final, where they expected to meet the Russians. But that matchup never materialized, as the Russians were upset by Yugoslavia, 63–62.

The final was a rematch against Yugoslavia, whom the United States had beaten by 15 points. This time the Yugoslavs were the underdogs, but they grabbed an early 11–6 lead before an overflow crowd of 25,000. The Americans rallied to lead at the half, 32–29. Then, in the second half, Haywood and White went on a scoring spree while the Americans' defense held the Yugoslavs without a field goal for the first seven minutes.

The United States won the game 65–50. Haywood had a game-high 23 points, 10 rebounds, and 5 blocked shots as he held the Yugoslav star, Cermak, to just 8 points. *The New York Times* referred to Haywood's night as "one of the greatest (individual performances) ever seen in the Olympic Games." And when it was over, Spencer Haywood's name had become as big as most of those who had boycotted the games.

The diminutive Globetrotters coach, Abe Saperstein

Globetrotters Formed Far From Harlem

The most surprising fact about the birth of the Harlem Globetrotters is that they were not formed in New York, as their name would imply, but rather in Chicago. Their founder, Abe Saperstein, had been born in London, the son of Polish immigrants who came to America when he was a child. Saperstein loved sports, but grew to a height of only 5′3″, so he began coaching.

In 1926, Saperstein became the coach of the Savoy Big Five, an all-black team that played its games in the Savoy Ballroom on Chicago's South Side. Before the year ended, the ballroom's owners decided that basketball was not bringing enough people into the dance hall. They asked the team to leave, planning to offer roller skating at the ballroom instead. The team decided to stick together and follow Saperstein's dream of taking the team on the road.

Saperstein himself created the new uniforms in his father's tailor shop, sewing new letters and gold stars onto the Savoy Big Five jerseys. They chose the name Harlem to make it clear that the team had only black players. And they chose "Globetrotters" to give the impression that they had taken on teams far and wide, although they hadn't played a single game outside Chicago.

On January 7, 1927, the five original Harlem Globetrotters and their coach Abe Saperstein left Chicago in an old model-T Ford and headed west fifty miles to the small town of Hinckley, Illinois. There they played their first game, defeating the local team. Their share of the gate receipts was a whopping $75, with each of the players receiving just over $10. Saperstein was given the rest for his multiple role as coach, manager, and driver.

That turned out to be one of their better nights in that first year of touring. At one game in Chicago, only twenty-seven people showed up, producing gate receipts of just over nine dollars. Saperstein settled for five dollars as the Globetrotters' share, enough to buy sandwiches and some gas. Similar disappointments greeted them in other locales, as basketball interest was simply not very high in the rural Midwest.

Times were tough, but the team managed to have fun despite the humiliations they had to endure in a largely segregated society. They impressed everyone with their basketball talents, doing all they could to win every game to build their reputation. In that first season, they played 117 games and won 101 of them. They had not yet developed the crowd-pleasing antics that we now expect of the Globetrotters, but those were soon to come.

The Globetrotters quickly learned that winning by a huge margin did not enhance their chances of being asked back the following year. Under the leadership of Inman Jackson, who joined the team in their second season, they developed the ballhandling routines that amazed the crowd and also provided needed rest for their tired legs. When a game ended, the local team had not been totally destroyed, and the crowd had been thoroughly entertained—a surefire guarantee for a return engagement.

The Globetrotters Conquer Berlin

In 1951, the Harlem Globetrotters were on an international tour that began at the Rose Bowl in Pasadena, California, where they set an American record by drawing over 31,000 fans for a basketball game. They later drew a crowd of over 50,000 in Brazil before moving on to Europe. With the Cold War brewing, the Globetrotters encountered a great deal of anti-American feeling while playing in France. But that was nothing compared to what had just happened in Germany.

American boxer Sugar Ray Robinson had recently fought a match in Germany that prompted so much antagonism toward America that bottle-throwing crowds began to riot. United States high commissioner to Germany John J. McCloy contacted the Globetrotters in Paris and asked them to help ease tensions by making a special appearance in Berlin's Olympic Stadium.

This was the same stadium in which Adolph Hitler had snubbed American

Jesse Owens in 1936. He had refused to shake the hand of a black man, even if he had just won four gold medals. But fifteen years later, the Globetrotters' reception would be far more cordial.

When the Globetrotters landed in Berlin, there was a mob of people surrounding their bus, putting the players more than slightly ill at ease. As it turned out, the Germans merely wanted to shake hands with the world-famous team.

On August 22, 1951, the largest crowd ever to see a basketball game, 75,000 people, poured into Olympic Stadium to watch a team that consisted entirely of black players and was owned by a Jew. The Germans loved every minute of it, roaring over the antics of Goose Tatum and Marques Haynes.

At halftime, there was a very special moment. A helicopter landed on the field, and out stepped a black man in a track suit. It was none other than Jesse Owens. Alongside the helicopter stood the mayor of West Berlin, Ludwig Shreiber, who greeted Owens by saying, "Fifteen years ago on this field Hitler refused to offer you his hand. Now I give you both of mine."

The crowd erupted into a thunderous ovation and cheered for five minutes, and Owens slowly ran one last lap around the track. Anti-American tension in Berlin had been greatly eased by the appearance of Owens, and by the team that the U.S. State Department began to refer to as the Ambassadors of Good Will—the Harlem Globetrotters. Forty years later, the Globetrotters are still playing that role wonderfully.

Pistons' Pitch Ends DeBusschere's Baseball Career

Now a member of the Basketball Hall of Fame, Dave DeBusschere is best remembered as a key forward on the New York Knicks championship teams in 1970 and 1973. A member of the NBA All-Defensive First Team for six consecutive years, DeBusschere came to the Knicks in December of 1968, in exchange for Walt Bellamy and Howard Komives. The Knicks could thank the Pistons not only for trading him to New York, but also for making sure that DeBusschere stayed in basketball a few years before.

A native of Detroit, DeBusschere was a two-sport star at Austin High School in the Motor City, leading his team to the city championship in both basketball and baseball. A hard-throwing right-handed pitcher, Dave continued to play both sports while earning a degree in marketing at the University of Detroit. Long before he graduated, he had scouts from both sports drooling.

In the spring of 1962, DeBusschere signed a contract with the White Sox that included a bonus reported to be somewhere between $70,000 and $160,000—big money for baseball in the early '60s. He immediately joined the Sox farm club at Savannah, where he went 10–1 with a glittering 2.49 earned run average. Late in the year he was called up to Chicago, a rare feat for a first-year pro. But DeBusschere was not just another rookie.

Meanwhile, the hometown Pistons also signed him as their first-round pick for a salary of $15,000. Dave had a solid rookie year, averaging 13 points a game in the regular season and 20 points in the playoffs.

DeBusschere enjoyed another fine baseball season in 1963, pitching in 24 games for the White Sox and finishing with a 3–4 record and a 3.09 ERA. Dave was a two-sport major leaguer and seemed happy playing both sports, but Pistons owner Fred Zollner wanted him for himself. And he got him, by offering Dave a huge raise, and the job of player-coach.

At the ripe age of 24, DeBusschere gave up baseball to become the youngest coach in NBA history. Saddled with a bad team, DeBusschere compiled a record of 79–143 in three seasons as player-coach. When he was finally freed of the burden of coaching, Dave's level of play climbed even higher, as he had the best rebounding year of his career. And the following season, when he was traded to the Knicks, he made the all-NBA second team.

DeBusschere went on to become the commissioner of the ABA and later the general manager of the Knicks—two more opportunities he might never have gotten if Fred Zollner hadn't lured him away from baseball forever.

Dave DeBusschere, a two-sport major leaguer

The First Televised Basketball Game

The first sport to be televised was baseball, beginning with a college game between Princeton and Columbia on May 17, 1939. Later that same year, television carried a boxing match at Yankee Stadium, a Dodgers-Reds doubleheader at Ebbets Field, and a number of football games.

In February of 1940, NBC took their cameras indoors to cover sports for the first time. Their first televised event was the AAU track championships at

Madison Square Garden. The next night they televised a hockey game between the New York Rangers and Montreal Canadiens. And then, on February 28, 1940, basketball received its first television coverage.

At the time, there were only about three hundred television sets in the country, all of them in the New York metropolitan area. Most of them had been given to prominent figures in the newspaper and advertising community. Others had been purchased by tavern owners for $660 apiece, with those astute barkeepers guessing correctly that curious patrons would crowd around the small screens.

Basketball's first telecast was a college doubleheader, matching Pittsburgh against Fordham in the first game, then Georgetown against NYU. The announcer was a relative unknown who called himself Bill Allen, although his real name was Allen William Walz. Allen had excelled in amateur athletics at NYU as captain of the football team and as an oarsman. But as an announcer, his experience was limited to some public-address announcing at football and baseball games.

As it turned out, Allen had a couple of real sleepers to call. In the first game, Pittsburgh easily disposed of Fordham 57–37. And with the Garden almost half empty, 9,657 fans cheered NYU to a 50–27 rout in the feature game.

The win by NYU was its eighteenth in a row, and at least the TV audience got to see it in its entirety. Not so the first game: For twenty minutes during the first half, the screen was completely black.

College Basketball's First National Champions

After the invention of basketball in December 1891, it didn't take long for colleges to sport their own teams. In February 1893 Vanderbilt fielded the first college team in the United States, and many other schools immediately followed suit. By the end of the year, there was already talk of holding a national championship. But given the travel difficulties of the time, regional championships were more feasible, and they were soon established in different parts of the country.

Two of the earliest leagues were formed in the East in 1901. The Intercollegiate League, the forerunner of the Ivy League, included Yale, Harvard, Princeton, Cornell, and Columbia, while the New England League consisted of Amherst, Holy Cross, Williams, Dartmouth, and Trinity.

The first intersectional play had already taken place in 1900 when Yale went on a western road swing, but there was no organized competition between teams from different parts of the country. When the first attempt at a national tournament finally arrived, it had nothing approaching a representative field.

Staged in conjunction with the 1904 Olympics at St. Louis, it was billed as the Olympic World's College Basket Ball Championship although it included only three teams. Hiram College of Ohio took home the gold medal, with the silver going to Wheaton College and the bronze to Latter Day Saints University (now Brigham Young).

Finally, the next year, one team had a legitimate claim to a national championship. The Eastern Intercollegiate League underwent a change in 1905, when charter member Harvard dropped out of the league. Since Pennsylvania had been added the year before, it was once again a five-team league. Totally unchanged, though, was the balance of power. For the second straight year, Columbia completed the season without losing a game.

Meanwhile, out west the teams had not yet formed conferences, but Chicago and Minnesota were the dominant teams. They were joined by Wisconsin, who featured Chris Steinmetz, the greatest scorer the game had ever seen. In a time when most teams were scoring about 20 points a game, Steinmetz set a record by scoring 50 points in one game. He also established another record by averaging 25.7 points a game during a season. Finally, he became the first college player to score 1,000 points in his career.

But not even Steinmetz could overcome Columbia's dominance. In a head-to-head meeting, Columbia defeated Wisconsin 21–15. To further cement their claim as the best team in the land, Columbia also knocked off Minnesota 27–15. They were thus considered the first true national champion—and rightly so.

Scoring star
Chris Steinmetz

The First National Collegiate Playoff

In 1905, Columbia was considered the first true national champion, having gone undefeated with victories over two of the best teams in the West. It was not until 1908, however, that the best of the East hooked up with the best of the West in a postseason playoff.

There was no doubt as to the best team in the East that year, as Pennsylvania won all eight of their games in the Eastern Intercollegiate League against conference foes Columbia, Yale, Cornell, Harvard, and Princeton. Overall, the Quakers went 23–2, and they finished the season with 22 consecutive wins.

The Western Intercollegiate League consisted of the Universities of Wisconsin, Minnesota, Illinois, Chicago, and Purdue. Their champion was not as clear-cut. Chicago and Wisconsin tied for first place with records of 7–1, and split the two games against each other.

A playoff for the conference title was held at Wisconsin, giving the Badgers the home-court edge. But Chicago had the bigger stars in 6′3″ center John Schommer and Pat Page, one of the game's quickest players. They also had the best coach of that era, Joseph Raycroft.

With 1,500 fans cheering for Wisconsin, Schommer and Page led Chicago to an 18–16 victory and the right to meet Pennsylvania for the national title. They beat Wisconsin on a last-minute shot by Page. They would need even greater heroics against Pennsylvania.

The national playoff would be a home-and-home series with the first game at Chicago. The home team beat Pennsylvania 21–18, as Page again made the game's most improbable shot, a desperation heave from between his legs as he was about to be tied up.

The second game, played in Philadelphia, was even tighter. Eight times the contest was tied before Chicago won it by a single point, 16–15, to nail down the national championship. This time it was Schommer who performed the miracle, by launching a last-second shot from beyond midcourt that went through to win the game.

That was not the end of Schommer's glory on the basketball court. The next year he became an All-American for the fourth consecutive year. During that season he had a streak of defensive excellence in which he held opposing centers to a total of only 4 baskets in a span of 9 games. And, several years later, John Schommer received credit for inventing the modern backboard. He was one of basketball's great Hall-of-Famers for more than just his on-court performances.

The New York Rens

If someone told you of a 1930s barnstorming team composed of seven black players that was considered the best basketball team in the world, you'd naturally assume it was the Harlem Globetrotters. But in fact, that championship unit was a club called the New York Rens.

Officially called the Renaissance Big Five, the Rens were founded in 1922 by a zealous fan named Bob Douglas, who wanted to call them the Spartans. Douglas made a deal for them to use the new Renaissance Casino Ballroom in Harlem—when it wasn't being used by the likes of Count Basie's band—so they became the Rens. And it wasn't long before black youngsters throughout the country dreamed of playing for the Rens.

The Rens, who preceded the Globetrotters in basketball history, became nationally prominent in 1926–27. That season, they split a six-game series against the original Celtics, who were considered the world's best team. By 1932 they were playing all their games on the road and winning almost all of them. When they added a seventh star to their roster that year, 6′5″ center "Wee" Willie Smith, they became very close to unbeatable.

The addition of Smith completed a lineup that soon became the world's best. In a four-year period beginning in 1932, the Rens won 473 games and lost only 49, with many of those losses due to blatantly prejudiced officiating. In the 1933–34 season, the Rens won 88 games in a row. And when they called them-

Rens captain
Clarence "Fat" Jenkins

selves World Champions, nobody disagreed.

During their four-year peak, the seven-man team remained intact. Needless to say, their teamwork was near perfect, and their stamina was unparalleled. Usually all five starters would play the entire game while the other two men got the night off.

Just who were these seven individuals?

First, there was Clarence "Fat" Jenkins, the Rens' captain and oldest player, who had joined the team back in 1924. Only 5′7″, but known as the "fastest man in basketball," Jenkins led a furious fast break and often drew double coverage to contain his driving layups.

Jenkins also starred in the Negro Baseball League, as did his backcourt mate Bill Yancey, the Rens' playmaker and defensive specialist. Yancey is now best known as a baseball scout whose many discoveries included Al Downing and Billy Bruton.

The Rens' other little man was Eyre "Bruiser" Saitch, another multisport star. Saitch was an outstanding tennis player, but never was allowed to test his game against the top white players. Saitch and John "Casey" Holt were the swingmen on the team, along with their flamboyant crowd pleaser, James "Pappy" Ricks.

The game's best shooter, Ricks would perform shooting exhibitions before and sometimes during the games. "Pappy" would often delight the crowd by shaking hands with himself above his head after his show had ended.

When the Rens would miss a shot, one of their two big men was often there to put in the rebound. Charles "Tarzan" Cooper, who was 6′4″, was called "the best center I ever saw," by Hall of Famer Joe Lapchick. But it was 6′5″ Wee Willie Smith who received credit for being the final piece of the puzzle that turned the Rens into world champions. Rens owner Bob Douglas brought Smith in from Cleveland in 1932, making Smith the only Ren who was not from New York or Philadelphia.

Completing the traveling party was road secretary Eric Illidge, who also drove the team bus. Illidge made sure the Rens received their rightful gate receipts, often refusing to let the players on the court until he had been paid the proper amount.

It took a special kind of talent and character to succeed against the type of prejudice the Rens encountered in the 1930s. The Rens traveled on their own bus, and often had to sleep on it, dining on cold cuts because hotels and restaurants refused to serve them. Their incredible record was achieved in spite of hostile fans and officials, and sometimes shifty promoters, who tried to shortchange them on their share of the gate.

In 1939, although the seven original stars were no longer together, the Rens won an official World Championship Tournament. They continued playing until 1949, and when the team disbanded, they sported an all-time record of 2,588–529.

Not surprisingly, the entire seven-man team of 1932–36 was later inducted as a unit into the Basketball Hall of Fame—a fitting testimony to one of the first great basketball dynasties!

The Mogul

When Eddie Gottlieb was inducted into the Basketball Hall of Fame in 1971 as a "contributor" to the sport, he was still active in the NBA. But his contributions to the growth of basketball date all the way back to 1918.

A native of Kiev, Russia, who came to America as a boy, Gottlieb first made his mark as the organizer and coach of the Sphas, a team representing the South Philadelphia Hebrew Association. Playing first in a city league and then in the Eastern League, the Sphas dominated their competition. When the American Basketball League was reorganized in 1933 as a regional circuit in the Northeast, Gottlieb's team joined up and won the first title. Featuring a lineup made up entirely of Jewish players, the Sphas went on to win 7 championships in the league's 13 years.

Gottlieb was one of his era's great promoters. He had a hand in professional wrestling, semipro football, and Negro baseball. He also helped organize overseas tours for the Harlem Globetrotters. These activities helped earn him the nickname "the Mogul." But his skills were best demonstrated in his promotion of the Sphas.

In the 1930s, the Sphas played home games every Saturday night at the Broadwood Hotel in Philadelphia. Fans would climb three flights of marble steps to get to their plush upholstered reserved seats in the ballroom. The place held 3,000 fans, and for thirty-five cents, spectators were promised a triple attraction—a basketball game, a dance, and a fight.

That's right. Before every game, Chickie Passion of the Sphas would start a fistfight with one of the opposing players. And, after the game, a dance was held, with another Sphas player, Gil Fitch, changing into a tuxedo and leading the band.

When pro basketball became truly major league after World War II, Eddie was a big part of it. In 1946, he helped found the Basketball Association of America, as coach of the Philadelphia Warriors. He soon bought the team from its owners for $25,000, and a few years later he helped work out the merger with the National Basketball League that created the NBA. He continued coaching the Warriors in the NBA through 1955, when he moved entirely to the front office and scored a major coup.

Wilt Chamberlain was then a high-school star in Philadelphia. Gottlieb convinced the NBA owners to grant him territorial rights to Chamberlain in 1959, when his college class would graduate, even if Wilt went to college outside of Philadelphia. Until then, territorial rights applied only to players who went to college in a team's geographic area. The addition of Wilt the Stilt, who attended Kansas University, ensured the success of the Warriors. When Gottlieb finally sold the team in 1962, the price was $850,000, or thirty-four times what he had paid for it.

The Warriors moved to San Francisco, and Gottlieb was hired to run the club for a few more years. When he retired, he continued working for the NBA for several years as the league's schedule maker. When Eddie died in 1979 at the age of eighty-one, he had helped shape the development of basketball, and had given over sixty years of his life to the game.

The First Championship in the NBA's Modern Era

The new rules implemented in 1954 sped up the game considerably and helped the teams who were suited to a fast-breaking style of play. Definitely not among those teams was the defending champion Minneapolis Lakers, a team that had won six championships in seven years. The Lakers used a deliberate, set-up offense designed to work the ball in to center George Mikan—no matter how long it took. Under the new rules, the Lakers would have to run with the rest of the teams, and Mikan decided to retire at the age of thirty to attend law school.

Without the league's top star, the Lakers fell to second in the West, behind the Fort Wayne Pistons. The Syracuse Nationals, the team they had beaten in the finals in Mikan's last year, became NBA champions.

Nats star
Dolph Schayes

When the rules changed for the 1954–55 season, Syracuse had a big advantage. In star forward Dolph Schayes, the Nationals had the most mobile of the league's big men, a great passer who could also drive with the ball from one end of the court to the other. And in the 1954 draft they picked up center Johnny Kerr, who would help Schayes control the boards and start the fast break.

During the regular season, the Nats went 43–29 to win the East by five games over the New York Knicks. They knocked off the Celtics in the Eastern playoff final, then hooked up with Fort Wayne in a dramatic final series.

The Pistons led three games to two but the last two games were in Syracuse, where the Nationals utilized the home-court advantage, winning Game Six to set up a deciding seventh game.

It turned out to be one of the greatest games the NBA had ever seen, with Syracuse rallying from a seventeen-point deficit in the first half. With a minute left it was tied at 91–91. Syracuse guard George King became the hero by sinking a free throw with twelve seconds to go, then stealing the ball to preserve the victory.

Syracuse had become the first champion of the NBA's modern era, but it was to be their only championship before the team moved to Philadelphia and became the 76ers in 1963.

Fort Wayne's fate was even darker. The Pistons lost in the finals again the following year, then moved to Detroit in 1957, where they finally won an NBA championship thirty-two years later.

Spencer Haywood Rewrites the Rules

The Spencer Haywood saga is a real Cinderella story. Born in Silver City, Mississippi, in 1949, Spencer earned his livelihood working in the cotton fields along with his nine brothers and sisters. Their father had died from working overly long hours as a carpenter, and their mother earned a meager wage scrubbing floors. At the age of thirteen, Spencer moved in with a brother in Chicago, and soon he got involved with gangs and guns. Fortunately, he was able to escape that environment.

While visiting in Detroit, Spencer ran into a man named Will Robinson, a coach at Detroit's Pershing High School. Robinson arranged for Spencer to live with a family in Detroit and attend Pershing, where he became a star in basketball and track.

Colleges throughout the country were after Spencer, but his reading skills were so poor he would have to attend a junior college first. Haywood became a Junior College All-American at Trinidad State in Colorado. Only nineteen years old, Spencer then led the 1968 US Olympic Team to a gold medal, which led to a whole new round of scholarship offers. Haywood chose the University of Detroit and proceeded to lead the nation in rebounding in 1969.

Rather than enter his junior year in college, Haywood jumped at an offer from the Denver Rockets of the ABA, a multiyear contract that would lift his family from poverty. The NBA was shocked, as they still adhered to their policy of prohibiting a college player from signing until his class had graduated. But the ABA rules allowed such a signing in the case of "extreme hardship," and Haywood certainly met their criteria.

Now fully grown at 6′9″, Haywood dominated the ABA, leading the league in scoring and rebounding, to win the Rookie of the Year and the MVP Awards. Following that season, Haywood decided to jump to Seattle of the NBA when the Supersonics made him a lucrative offer. But the NBA refused to let him play because his college class had not yet graduated and he had not gone through the NBA draft. Haywood and the Supersonics then filed an antitrust suit against the NBA, and a judge eventually granted an injunction allowing him to play for Seattle.

Haywood played 33 games that year and averaged over 20 points a game. In March, a federal judge ruled that the NBA draft was illegal if it did not provide some way for a player to turn pro whenever he wants to. Haywood and the Sonics settled their suit against the league out of court; the settlement allowed the Sonics to keep him. More important was the judge's ruling, which ultimately forced the NBA to admit a so-called hardship case before his college class has graduated.

Spencer Haywood went on to play nine years in the NBA. He was a first-team All-Star twice and a second-team All-Star twice. But his biggest contribution to the pro game probably occurred not on the court, but in the courtroom.

The NBA's Smallest All-Star

Long before Calvin Murphy and Spud Webb came along, it was Slater Martin who proved that there is a place in the NBA for an average-sized human being. At Jefferson Davis High School in Houston, Texas, Martin was only 5′7″ when he led the school to back-to-back Texas state titles in 1942 and 1943.

A self-described 5′10″ "gunner" at the University of Texas, Martin left the Longhorns as the leading scorer in school history. He set a Southwest Conference record with 49 points in one game, but it was his defense that attracted the pros. Martin always guarded the opposition's top scorer, even if that player was six inches taller.

The powerhouse Minneapolis Lakers drafted Martin in 1949, primarily to defend against the league's top guards and to get the ball to George Mikan and their other big men. As for scoring, forget it—Martin as a rookie averaged only 4 points a game. But the Lakers won the NBA title, one of four that Martin celebrated in seven years with the Lakers.

Known to his teammates as "Dugie," Martin was one of only two NBA players to wear contact lenses in those days. Had he worn glasses, they likely would have been shattered by frustrated opponents. Bob Cousy described Martin's defense as the toughest he ever played against, with the speed, stamina, and intensity to sustain the effort for forty-eight minutes.

Martin never averaged as much as 14 points a game, but, beginning in 1954, he was a Second-Team NBA All-Star five years in a row. In the midst of that All-Star run, Martin was traded.

In the fall of 1956, Martin was holding out for more money. The Lakers, who needed a big man to replace Mikan, traded Martin to the Knicks for Walter Dukes. Then, in a prearranged deal, the Knicks shipped him to the Lakers' Western Division rivals, the St. Louis Hawks, in exchange for forward Willie Naulls.

Slater's job remained the same, only now he would be feeding the ball to the Hawks' star, Bob Pettit. Hawks owner Ben Kerner expected to win it all, and when the team had a losing record in January, he fired coach Red Holzman and named Martin player-coach.

It was a great idea, except for one thing: Martin did not want to coach, he wanted to concentrate on playing. After just eight games, Martin threatened to go home if Kerner didn't come up with another coach. Martin recommended

University of Texas "gunner" Slater Martin

Hawks' bench-warmer Alex Hannum, who had been doing most of the real coaching when Martin was out on the court. Kerner took his advice and named Hannum coach.

Hannum turned out to be a huge success, and the Hawks went all the way to the NBA finals, where they lost the seventh game in double overtime, with Martin playing the entire fifty-eight minutes. The next year, the Hawks defeated the Celtics in the finals, and Slater Martin had his fifth championship.

Martin retired in 1960 with a career scoring average of only 9.8 points a game. Unfortunately, his tenacious defense and commitment to winning do not appear in any record book. However, anyone who played with him or against him knows he was one of the fiercest competitors to ever play the game.

The Birth of the Behind-the-Back Dribble

Today we take the behind-the-back dribble for granted. Even the big men, given some open court, will occasionally flash this popular move. But until the 1940s, it was generally unseen and unheard of.

Little Bob Davies changed all that. A five-foot-tall high-school guard who had been benched in junior high because of his size, Davies first saw the fancy dribble in a basketball movie, in which Hank Luisetti performed a similar stunt in slow motion. Davies began practicing the move at increasingly faster speeds. After three years of rehearsal, Davies unveiled what would become his trademark in his final year of high school in Harrisburg, Pennsylvania.

Davies went on to Seton Hall University as a shortstop on a baseball scholarship, and even signed an option with the Boston Red Sox to play for them after college. A walk-on in basketball, Davies led the freshman team to a victory over the varsity. By now he had grown to an even six feet and soon became one of the nation's best backcourt men.

Using the behind-the-back dribble at least once a game, Davies thrilled the crowds as he led Seton Hall to 43 straight wins and was named All-American twice. When asked later about his offensive strategy, his coach, Hall-of-Famer Honey Russell, replied, "I gave the ball to Davies and that was my offense." When Davies introduced the behind-the-back dribble to the Madison Square Garden crowd during the NIT in 1941, his reputation was forever established as the father of the move. But the pros would not embrace it as warmly as the fans did.

After leaving Seton Hall in 1942, Bob Davies served in the US Navy until 1945, when he joined the Rochester Royals of the NBL. The next year he also signed on to coach basketball and baseball at Seton Hall. The dual role enabled him to earn the staggering sum of $15,000 a year. But could he handle the mental and physical strain?

In one stretch, Davies had to sleep on a train thirteen nights in a row, but his play did not appear to suffer. He led the Royals to the league championship in

1946 and 1947, winning the MVP Award as well in 1947. That was the year he also coached his Seton Hall team to a record of 24–3.

The one frustration for Davies was the refusal of his professional coaches and owners to let him dribble behind his back. They felt it made the other players look bad, and it took several years for them to change their minds.

But Davies stayed around long enough to win many of them over, playing ten pro seasons and winning all-league honors seven times. In 1951, he led the Royals to the seventh game of the NBA finals against the Knicks. In the final minute, Davies drove to the basket, was fouled by Dick McGuire, and sank the two free throws that won the game, giving him 20 points for the night.

Davies used the set shot his entire career, a traditionalist in that regard. But when it came to ballhandling, he was a true pioneer.

Pro Basketball's First Great Shooter

It would be nearly impossible today for an NBA team to uncover a great talent who is totally unknown to everyone else. But back in the 1940s it could happen, and it did in the case of Joe Fulks. Born in Kutawa, Kentucky, Fulks had played college ball for little Murray State Teachers College in his home state. He'd then joined the US Marines for a four-year tour of duty during World War II.

Fulks played a lot of basketball in the service and faced a number of college All-Americans, an experience that convinced him that he could play pro ball. Also convinced was Petey Rosenberg, a former pro player who watched Fulks play at Pearl Harbor. Rosenberg recommended him to his old boss, Eddie Gottlieb of the Philadelphia Warriors, who quickly signed "Jumpin' Joe" to a pro contract upon his return home.

Fulks entered pro ball in 1946 for the first season of the Basketball Association of America, which later became the NBA. At the age of twenty-five, he was older than most rookies and much better, too. Fulks scored 25 points in the Warriors' first game, and went on to win the league scoring championship with an average of 23 points a game—nearly 7 points a game higher than the league's second-leading scorer. Fulks also led the Warriors to the championship, firing in 34 points in the deciding game of the playoffs.

Most of the game's high scorers in those days were big men, but Fulks was a skinny forward who stood only 6′5″. He scored with pro basketball's first great jump shot, which some referred to as an "ear shot," since Joe seemed to release the ball off his ear. Fans would often gaze at Fulks's point totals in disbelief, especially one day in 1949.

Big George Mikan had entered the league the previous year and had wrestled the scoring championship away from Fulks. But Jumpin' Joe saw to it that Mikan would not erase him entirely from the record book. On February 10, 1949, in a game against the Indianapolis Jets, Fulks delighted the Philadelphia fans with a 63-point outburst. He hit with turnaround jumpers, driving shots with both hands, and occasional set shots as well. Fulks's 63 points was recognized as the NBA record for ten years, until Elgin Baylor broke it by a single point in 1959.

Fulks played a total of eight years with the Warriors, retiring in 1954 at the age of thirty-three. His career was shorter than some because of his late start in pro ball. His detractors said that he was slow, and not very good on defense. But, as pro basketball's first great shooter and the pioneer of the jump shot, Jumpin' Joe Fulks earned a place in the Basketball Hall of Fame.

Jump shot pioneer Joe Fulks

An All-Star On and Off the Court

Imagine one man winning eleven championship rings in professional basketball—four as a player, three as a coach, and four as a team executive. Imagine him winning those titles with four different teams in three different leagues.

Sound farfetched? Maybe it does, but those are the actual accomplishments of Bill Sharman. However, Sharman's achievements go way beyond simply winning championships.

As a player in the '50s, Sharman was a 6′2″ guard who could not even dunk. But he was a deadly jump shooter who earned all-league honors seven times, including four straight first-team selections. He was the best free throw shooter of his era, leading the league seven times, still the NBA record. His career free-throw percentage (.883) is third best in NBA history.

Most important, Sharman was a great clutch player. Celtics coach Red Auerbach felt Sharman was the man he could always count on to make the right play when he needed it. In recognition of his all-around excellence, Sharman was one of ten men named to the NBA Silver Anniversary Team in 1971.

Sharman was not flamboyant, but one of his shots will never be forgotten. With time running out in the 1955 NBA All-Star Game, Sharman flung a long pass from beneath his own basket. It was too high for its intended target, Bob Cousy, but wound up in the basket for a 70-foot field goal, the longest in All-Star Game history.

After retiring as a player in 1961, Sharman was hired to coach the Los Angeles Jets of the new American Basketball League. Although his team folded in mid-season and resurfaced as the Cleveland Pipers, Sharman held the club together and won the title.

He later coached the San Francisco Warriors for two years, then jumped to the American Basketball Association, where he took the Utah Stars to a title in 1971. After that success, he was hired to coach the Los Angeles Lakers, a team of superstar talents who had been to the NBA finals seven times and never won.

Sharman somehow blended the team into a cohesive unit that won its first title. One of his innovations was the game-day "shootaround," an informal but mandatory workout. When Sharman first announced that the team would practice at 11 a.m. on game day, Wilt Chamberlain complained that he was not even out of bed by them. But the practice worked, and it is now accepted procedure by teams everywhere.

Sharman was also one of the first coaches to scout his opponents in great detail, guarding against any surprise that another team might spring. And he employed a system of fines and bonuses for mistakes and accomplishments that helped bring his teams together.

Sharman moved up to the Lakers' front office in 1976, and helped bring the 3-point shot to the NBA. He also engineered many of the trades and signings that have made the Lakers a dominant team. Sharman retired as the Lakers' president after their 1988 championship, with his voice almost completely blown out from years of hollering at referees. But he left intact a legacy that may be unequaled in professional basketball history.

The Star Center Who Was Never Good Enough

Big men averaging 20 points and 13 rebounds a game are few and far between in the NBA today. Someone averaging those figures over a span of thirteen years would be considered one of the all-time greats. Yet Walt Bellamy, whose statistics those are, never even made a single postseason NBA All-Star team.

Bellamy's lack of honors stemmed mostly from the era in which he played. Bellamy broke into the league in 1961, when a couple of guys named Russell and Chamberlain had a lock on the All-Star berths. And he was still around when Abdul-Jabbar entered the NBA.

The one honor that Bellamy captured easily was the Rookie of the Year Award in 1961–62. Walt had been the first pick in the NBA draft, a selection that was granted to the expansion Chicago Packers when they entered the league. The rookie from Indiana University received a big offer from the Cleveland team in the new American Basketball League, but chose the established league instead.

At 6′11″ and 245 pounds, Bellamy was considered a talent in the class of Russell and Chamberlain, and he confirmed that judgment by averaging 31.6 points a game as a rookie. There were some tough times, such as the first night he faced Chamberlain, when he suffered the indignity of having four consecutive shots blocked by Wilt the Stilt. But in his first meeting with Russell, Walt more than held his own, scoring 21 points against the defensive master of the NBA.

Bellamy's problem was his inability to sustain that level of performance on a consistent basis. His scoring average dropped in each of the next six years, and his sometimes lethargic air made it appear that he was just going through the motions. Not so, claimed Bellamy. "I try," he maintained. "Believe me. But sometimes it can't happen."

In his first four NBA seasons, Bellamy never averaged under 24 points and 14 rebounds, but his team, which moved from Chicago to Baltimore, never had a winning record. In November 1965, hoping to add needed depth, Baltimore traded Bellamy to the Knicks for Johnny Green, John Egan, Jim "Bad News" Barnes, and cash. The move backfired on the Bullets, who actually got worse the following season. But the Knicks, who had been just as bad as Baltimore when the deal was made, began to improve.

With Bellamy at center, the Knicks made the playoffs the next two years, and they posted a winning record for the first time in nine years. Bellamy combined with young Willis Reed, who had switched for forward, to give New York two of the league's top rebounders. But Reed's future was clearly at center, and when the right deal came along, the Knicks sent big Walter packing again.

One-time Rookie of the Year Walt Bellamy

This time he headed to Detroit, in exchange for forward Dave DeBusschere in December 1968. The trade allowed Reed to flourish at center, and the Knicks acquired the true forward they badly needed. The very next year, New York won the NBA championship.

As for Bellamy, he joined a bad Piston team, which did not get any better. Then he was traded in 1970 to an Atlanta team which was only slightly better. When he retired in 1974, he had played for only three teams with winning records in thirteen years. Not only had he never won a league championship, he had never even been to the finals.

While the trade from New York forced Walt to leave the best team he ever played for, it also enabled him to set an NBA record. Because of the team schedules that season, Bellamy was able to appear in 88 games. That's a record that may never be broken. It's also, unjustly, the only mark of any enduring distinction that this great center will ever own.

He'd Rather Be an Engineer

An honor student in chemical engineering who attended Purdue on an academic scholarship, Terry Dischinger was an unexpected surprise on the court for the Boilermakers. Despite a grueling schedule that allowed him less than four hours of sleep a night, the 6′6″ forward led the Big Ten in scoring as a sophomore. He set seven school-scoring records with an accurate outside shot and a willingness to hit the boards well, although his slender frame carried only 190 pounds.

After that season, Dischinger made the 1960 US Olympic Team at the age of nineteen, the youngest man ever to play Olympic basketball for this country. He ended up as the top scoring forward on the team, trailing only Oscar Robertson and Jerry West in overall scoring as the Americans easily won the gold medal in Rome.

Having already experienced what many consider the thrill of a lifetime, Terry returned to Purdue for two more outstanding seasons, finishing with Big Ten records for points in one season and points in a three-year career. He also had the biggest single game (52 points) in conference history, and he was on everyone's All-America team. With the NBA beckoning, Dischinger decided to forego pro basketball to pursue a career in engineering, fearing that he might forget all that he had learned in college.

Dischinger was bypassed in the first round of the 1962 NBA draft, but the Chicago Zephyrs made him the first selection of the second round. He had already accepted a job with the Phillips Petroleum Company, but the Zephyrs came up with a creative offer that got Terry's attention. To lure him away from his new job, the Zephyrs found Dischinger an engineering job in Chicago, which he could work at during the summers. With that obstacle cleared, the team also had to deal with Terry's desire to complete a few courses for his degree at Purdue. In what had to be the most unusual rookie contract ever, the Zephyrs agreed to let Dischinger skip road games if they interfered with his studies.

This unusual concession must have been scoffed at by other NBA owners, and in fact, Dischinger played in only 57 games that season. By midseason, however, nobody was laughing, as Dischinger was the only rookie selected to play in the All-Star game. And when the season ended, Dischinger had a 25.5-point average, an NBA record for field-goal percentage by a forward (51.7%) and the Rookie of the Year Award.

It was one of the best rookie seasons in NBA history, and it turned out to be the best year of Dischinger's career. He scored 20 points a game the next season, then was traded to a terrible Detroit team. The following year he entered the military, and when he returned to the Pistons two years later, he had lost his shooting touch. Terry played six more years in the NBA, but he averaged only about 10 points a game.

He retired to a career in engineering with an Olympic gold medal and an NBA Rookie of the Year Award. In Terry Dischinger's basketball career, the best definitely came first.

Billy McGill, with Chicago general manager Frank Lane

From College Superstar to NBA Failure

In the spring of 1962, the Chicago Zephyrs had the first pick in the draft after going 18–62 in their first NBA season. The available college stars included future pro standouts Zelmo Beaty, Dave DeBusschere, and John Havlicek. But with the very first pick, Chicago coach Jack McMahon selected Billy "the Hill" McGill.

A 6′9″ center out of Utah, McGill had led the country in scoring with an average of 38.8 points a game, at the time the second highest average ever in college ball. McGill had grown up in a Los Angeles ghetto and had led Jefferson High School to city championships in three of his four years. He was dubbed Bill the Hill by a sportswriter who saw him play in tenth grade, when at 6′8″, his shot was virtually unstoppable.

McGill used a unique jump hook, which he fired from the baseline with his back to the basket, a forerunner of the now familiar "sky hook." At Utah he was instructed to shoot as often as possible, and the strategy paid off. As a junior, McGill led his team to the final four of the NCAA tournament. But as a pro, McGill wouldn't be the one to take all the shots. And he was unable to adjust to a lesser role.

Billy the Hill was so accustomed to shooting that he initially wanted the Zephyrs to pay him by the point. He was finally persuaded to accept a regular salary instead, which probably kept him from going broke. The Zephyrs already had a high-scoring center, Walt Bellamy, who had finished second in the league in scoring behind Wilt Chamberlain the year before, and it was Bellamy who got most of the playing time and most of the shots.

Playing behind Bellamy, McGill averaged less than ten minutes per game, and although he shot a fine .513 from the field, he averaged just 7.4 points a contest. Confused by his new role, the sensitive rookie who had always been shy around people, became almost totally withdrawn.

The next year, McGill was traded to the Knicks and began to come into his own. Playing almost twenty-five minutes a game, he averaged 15 points. But then the Knicks drafted future All-Star Willis Reed and shipped McGill to St. Louis, receiving in return only a second-round draft choice and cash.

The trade shattered McGill's confidence, and he played poorly and sparingly for the Hawks. A month into the season he was cut, and he went to play in the Continental League. Late in the season, the Lakers signed him and Billy the Hill headed home to Los Angeles.

In a strange move that was designed to save money, the Lakers didn't take McGill with them when they went on the road. Instead, they left him at home to work on his shot. Unfortunately, it was his defense, rebounding, and passing that really needed improvement—skills which he had never developed at Utah, where scoring was all they asked of him.

McGill was on the Lakers' traveling squad in the playoffs, but he rarely played as they reached the finals and lost to Boston. The following year he tried out for the Warriors, but he failed to make the team. McGill resurfaced in 1968 in the ABA and averaged 10 points over two seasons before calling it quits at the age of thirty.

The NBA career of Billy the Hill lasted all of 159 games, proof positive that it takes more than a good shot to make it in the NBA.

A Shameful Waste of Talent

Jack Molinas was one of college basketball's greatest players in the 1950s. A 6′6″ forward at Columbia University, Molinas had all the tools. He was quick and strong, a fine shooter and rebounder with great instincts and intelligence. While at Columbia, Molinas rewrote the school record book. He averaged 18 points a game and set a school mark that still stands with a 31-rebound performance against Brown. But he received additional notoriety for a less admirable act.

During his sophomore year, Molinas was suspended for a semester for hurling a glass out a window. He made up the lost time by attending classes during the summer, though, and when he left Columbia in 1953, he became the first-round draft choice of the NBA's Fort Wayne Pistons.

In the first half of his rookie NBA season, Molinas was a standout, and was selected to play in the 1954 All-Star Game at Madison Square Garden. But ten days before the big event Molinas was scratched, not only from the All-Star Game but from the NBA.

Back in December 1953 NBA commissioner Maurice Podoloff had been informed of gambling rumors concerning Molinas. After an investigation, Podoloff personally questioned Molinas, who admitted that he had occasionally placed small wagers, but only on his own team to win.

Having seen the damage to college basketball caused by the scandal of 1951, Podoloff acted quickly. He expelled Molinas from the league, noting that NBA contracts specifically prohibited all forms of betting on league games. No criminal actions were filed against Molinas, but he would no longer earn a $9,600 salary as an NBA player.

After his banishment from pro basketball, Jack went to law school and became a successful attorney, but he still tried unsuccessfully to win reinstatement by the NBA. Instead, his return to basketball came as a key figure in a new wave of college basketball scandals in 1961. Molinas was found to be the chief liaison between the gamblers and the players in a scheme involving forty-seven players at colleges stretching from NYU all the way to Mississippi State.

As it turned out, Molinas had also been involved in fixing games while at Columbia, but he was so good at it that he was never caught, or even investigated. This time, however, he was not so lucky.

For his role in the 1961 scandal, Molinas served four years in a federal prison. When he got out, he continued to become involved in questionable ventures, including pornographic movies, and was soon making a lot of money. Then, in August 1975, it all came to a sudden end when he was found executed in mobster fashion with a bullet in the head.

Jack Molinas was only forty-three years old when he died. His NBA career consisted of just 29 games. In retrospect, the decision to throw him out was probably one of the best moves the league ever made.

"Hot" Rod Hundley's Colorful World

Described by some as the court jester, and by others as the white Globetrotter, "Hot" Rod Hundley was one of the most brilliant showmen ever to grace a basketball court. But his career will always be regarded as one of unfulfilled potential.

A highly prized high-school star from Charleston, West Virginia, Hundley was set to enter North Carolina State in 1953 when the NCAA announced sanctions against the school. Hundley settled instead for the University of West Virginia, and he proceeded to put the Mountaineers into the national spotlight.

A slender 6′4″ forward with a blond crewcut, Hundley set an NCAA record for points by a sophomore, hitting shots with both hands from all imaginable locations as the Mountaineeers won the Southern Conference title. But Hot Rod became famous more for his crowd-pleasing antics than for his scoring prowess. Once his team had a big lead, Hot Rod would go into his one-man act, spinning the ball on his fingers, sometimes dribbling it with his knees, then punching it into the basket, all the while chomping on a wad of bubble gum.

One of his favorite tricks was to offer the ball to an opponent with his outstretched right hand, only to flip it over his shoulder and catch it behind his back with his left hand. He would also shoot free throws with his back to the basket. Longtime referee Lou Eisenstein called him "the best crowd pleaser I've ever seen in college basketball."

But he was far more than just a clown. His coach at West Virginia, Fred Schaus, considered him the best all-around player in college basketball, and believed that Rod could become "a taller Bob Cousy." The *Wheeling Intelligencer* stated, "Hot Rod has given West Virginia more publicity than any other athlete with the possible exception of Sam Snead." And after leading West Virginia to a 25–5 record in 1957, his senior year, Hundley was a first-round draft choice of the Cincinnati Royals, who immediately traded him to the Minneapolis Lakers.

A man-about-town whose off-the-court exploits were legendary, Hundley put together a mediocre NBA career with the Lakers that lasted only six years, most of them as a bench-warmer. He averaged only 8.4 points a game, as he never put in the hard work that might have elevated his game. However, he remained a crowd pleaser, causing Laker fans to stay until the end of one-sided games, when

"Hot" Rod Hundley traded the basketball for the microphone.

Hot Rod would come off the bench and put on his show. Once he sank a hook shot for a free throw—the sort of move that thrilled the fans but not opposing players, and occasionally led to fistfights with humiliated opponents.

Known for wearing bizarre color combinations and flashy shoes, Hundley once gave *Sports Illustrated* a list of his favorite night spots in NBA cities. And when his autobiography *Clown* was published, his ex-wife joked, "If all his old girlfriends buy it, it will be a best seller." She might have included his bartenders, too.

One of the league's most quotable players, Hundley joked that "my biggest thrill came when Elgin Baylor and I combined for 73 points at Madison Square Garden. Elgin had 71 of them." And, on receiving a salary of only $10,000 as a first-round draft choice, Hot Rod says, "Every time I see my mother, I ask her, 'Why didn't you wait?' "

Now the radio-TV voice of the Utah Jazz, Hundley has worked harder at becoming a good broadcaster than he ever did as a pro player. His self-deprecating admission of this is best demonstrated in a recent comment about Ralph Sampson: "He's the most overrated player since me."

The Greatest High-School Teams Ever

The longest winning streak in NBA history is 33 games by the 1971–72 Los Angeles Lakers. UCLA's famous 88-game streak in the early '70s is the longest in major college basketball. As impressive as these two streaks may be, they both pale in comparison to high-school basketball's longest win streak.

It lasted over five years and two months, as the team from Passaic (New Jersey) High School won an incredible 159 games in a row, beginning on December 17, 1919, and ending on February 6, 1925. During the streak, Passaic outscored their opponents by an average of 59–20, almost tripling the point total of their opposition (9,435–3,236).

The streak finally ended in a game against Hackensack, also from New Jersey, in a hotly contested game that ended in a 39–35 score. By that time, Passaic had strung together five consecutive perfect seasons, which remains the national boys high school record.

Passaic's star player for most of that time, John Roosma, went on to star at West Point, where he led the Cadets to one undefeated season (31–0) and a career record of 73–13 as a collegian. Roosma later starred for several military teams, became a referee for college games, and earned enshrinement in the Basketball Hall of Fame.

His coach at Passaic, Professor Ernest Blood, was also inducted into the Hall of Fame. In his ten years at Passaic, his teams ran up a record of 200–1 and won seven state championships. Later, as a college coach at West Point and Clarkson College, his teams compiled a mark of 56–7.

Passaic's streak remains in a class by itself among boys teams. But that streak was surpassed by a high-school girls team from Baskin, Louisiana. The Baskin girls won 218 straight games in a streak that started in 1947 and ended in 1953.

The most famous girls team is one that made its mark after its players had graduated. For twenty-five years, the best women's basketball team in North America was the Edmonton (Alberta) Commercial Grads, made up entirely of players who had graduated from the same high school in Canada. Between 1915 and 1940, the Grads won 522 games and lost only 20 as they traveled throughout the United States, Canada, and Europe.

The Grads were coached by John Percy Page, who insisted that his players conduct themselves "like ladies" at all times. The players all had jobs, mostly as teachers and secretaries, and any player who got married was automatically dropped from the team. They even had a farm system to replace those who left for a more traditional family life. Amazingly, only thirty-eight different players appeared in the Grads' lineup during their twenty-five-year existence.

The Grads practiced for hours, and had to play their home games outdoors since they didn't have a gym. Their longest winning streak was "only" 147 games in a row. Not quite up to the standard set by the Passaic boys and the Baskin girls, but not bad for a group of high-school hoopsters who just didn't want to give up the game.

Furman's 100-Point Man

Born Franklin Delano Selvy on the day in 1932 that FDR was first elected president, Frank Selvy put Baptist Furman College on the basketball map because nobody else wanted him. A six-foot center from the small coal-mining town of Corbin, Kentucky, Selvy was not highly regarded in high school. Coach Adolph Rupp told him that he was too short to play for Kentucky. But Furman coach Lyle Alley liked him in an All-Star game and invited him for a tryout.

Selvy journeyed down to Greenville, South Carolina, where he opened the eyes of the Furman coaches by sinking four hook shots left-handed, then four more with his right hand. Frank was given the first full basketball scholarship ever at Furman, the only scholarship offer he received, and one that made Alley appear to be a genius. In Alley's words, "He had a way of making things look so easy, the way a champion does."

National scoring champion, that is. Selvy led the nation as a junior in 1953, averaging 29.5 points a game. He repeated the feat in 1954, setting an NCAA record with an average of 41.7 points. Although he grew to only 6′2½″, Selvy had great spring in his legs and always took the center jump, usually winning it against taller opponents. He was a deadly shooter with either hand, he could drive or hook it in, and he could hit his jump shot after a 180° spin in midair. Alley later recalled, "He had the most remarkable coordination I've ever seen in a human being."

Selvy played forward, guard, or center, wherever he was needed, and averaged 14 rebounds a game his senior year. It was as a center that Frank had his most

Record-setting Frank Selvy

memorable game on February 13, 1954. About five hundred folks had made the four-hour drive from Corbin to watch him for the first time. They weren't disappointed.

Selvy's hometown fans witnessed the greatest individual performance in major college basketball history, as "Fabulous" Frank pumped in 100 points. Selvy destroyed the old record of 73 points set by Bill Mlkvy of Temple, and set an all-time NCAA career scoring record on the same night. In winnıng 149–95 Furman also set a one-game record for most points.

Selvy was sometimes guarded by three men, and he said later that he didn't realize he was going for a record until he already had it. Frank scored 40 points in the first half, and Coach Alley told his team to keep feeding Selvy in the second half. When Mlkvy's record of 73 points was broken, the PA announcer started counting off the points each time Selvy scored. By this time, Selvy was the only Furman starter still in the game, and he just went right on scoring.

He finished with 41 field goals in 72 attempts, a nifty 57% field goal percentage. He also hit 18 of 21 from the free throw line. Ironically, Selvy was known as a modest, quiet team player, and often refrained from using his best moves for fear of showing off.

But on this night, Selvy used all his moves to land in the college record book. At season's end, he was named the nation's College Player of the Year.

The Shot Selvy Failed to Make

The 1954 College Player of the Year who had twice led the nation in scoring and once scored 100 points in a game, Frank Selvy was the first choice in the NBA draft in August 1954. The 6′2″ guard was chosen by the Baltimore Bullets ahead of such stars as Bob Pettit and Gene Shue, and it appeared to be an excellent choice as Selvy made an easy transition to the pros.

Fabulous Frank led the league in scoring for the first month, only to have the financially troubled Bullets fold in late November. Selvy's contract was assigned to the Milwaukee Hawks, where he picked up right where he had left off in Baltimore. Selvy was selected to play in the NBA All-Star Game, and he finished fifth in the league in scoring with an average of 19 points a game.

What appeared to be the dawning of an NBA star was abruptly interrupted when Selvy was drafted into the army after 17 games of his second pro season. He spent eighteen months in Germany, during which he injured his left knee and suffered back trouble. When he rejoined the Hawks in 1957, Frank had lost his shooting touch. With the team well stocked at the guard positions, Selvy got little opportunity to regain his shot, and he asked to be traded. The Hawks obliged, sending him to the Lakers.

By then, Selvy had lost his confidence along with his shot and his timing. In the next two years he was traded to New York, Syracuse, and then back to the Lakers, averaging only 9.5 points and twenty minutes a game. But returning to the Lakers was a lucky move, as coach Fred Schaus had a new role in mind for college basketball's greatest scorer. Schaus already had two big scorers in Jerry West and Elgin Baylor, and he saw Selvy as a valuable veteran who could help the team with his ballhandling and defense.

Schaus told Selvy to forget about scoring, and assigned him to cover the opposition's top guard. He went head-to-head with the likes of Oscar Robertson and Bob Cousy as the Lakers battled to the NBA finals in 1962 and 1963. Known to his younger teammates as Pops, the quiet, low-key Selvy was lauded by Schaus for his consistency. In 1962, Selvy raised his scoring average to 14.7 points, but Schaus pointed out, "It's the other things he does that makes him so valuable to our cause."

Although Selvy had indeed made a successful comeback as a defensive standout, his NBA career will be best remembered for a shot he failed to sink. In the 1962 NBA Finals, the Lakers and Celtics were tied in the closing seconds of Game Seven at the Boston Garden. Playing for the last shot, Laker guard Rod Hundley passed to Selvy, who put up a short jumper that would not fall through and rolled off the rim. Instead of winning the NBA title on that shot, the Lakers were forced into overtime and lost the game. Selvy later claimed that Cousy had fouled him, but no one remembers that now. And they don't remember that it was a Selvy basket that had tied the game. They remember instead the potential championship-winning shot that missed, and the high-scoring career that might have been.

The Magic of "The Pearl"

Those who experienced the joy of watching Earl "the Pearl" Monroe will never forget his unmatched flair, his dazzling array of moves, his ability to get off a shot or an accurate pass regardless of how well covered he appeared to be. But unlike "Dr. J" or Michael Jordan, Monroe was unstoppable despite a creaky pair of legs that prevented him from getting very far off the ground. Often he had the defender so badly fooled that Earl could get off a shot without leaving the floor at all.

Earl Monroe

Oddly enough, Monroe did not play much basketball growing up in Philadelphia, preferring soccer instead. He began playing basketball in junior high school and improved rapidly, making the all-city team as a senior in high school. But Earl was tired of school and upon graduating, took a job as a shipping clerk, despite scholarship offers from Winston-Salem and several other colleges.

One day Earl decided he was ready for college, and when he left work for lunch he never came back, driving down to North Carolina that afternoon. Under coach Clarence Gaines at Winston-Salem, Monroe became an offensive superstar. As a senior in 1967, he averaged 41.5 points, hitting over 60% of his shots from the field.

The Detroit Pistons had the first choice in the NBA draft that year and used it to take Jimmy Walker of Providence. Drafting second, the Baltimore Bullets took Monroe. The Pearl quickly became an NBA star, winning the Rookie-of-the-Year Award as he averaged 24 points a game to finish fourth in the league in scoring.

The next year, Monroe finished second in the league with a 25.8-point average and made the first all-star team at the end of the season. The Bullets won the Eastern Conference regular-season title that year, and advanced to the NBA finals in 1971. But Earl's aching feet and knees were becoming a serious problem, and in November 1971 he was traded to the New York Knicks for Dave Stallworth, Mike Riordan, and cash. That trade helped bring the Knicks an NBA championship two years later.

Earl the Pearl played little in his first year with the Knicks, as he underwent an operation to remove bone spurs from his foot. But when he returned in 1972–73, he became a key ingredient in the Knicks' second NBA title. While his scoring average fell to 15.5 points a game, Monroe teamed with Walt Frazier in a dream backcourt, and he adapted more easily to the Knicks' team concept than anyone could have predicted.

Monroe's arthritic knees continued to give him trouble, but he played effectively until the age of thirty-five. With a level of showmanship unmatched in his era, the Pearl continued to be a fan favorite until the day he retired. Earl Monroe must be considered one of the best one-man shows in NBA history.

The Men in the Striped Shirts

There is no disputing the fact that the most thankless job in the basketball arena belongs to the referees. Fans berate them, coaches scream their lungs out at them, and players often react to their judgments with hostile glares.

Actually, referees have it a lot better now than they used to. In the first year of the NBA, 1949–50, the refs were often criticized publicly by coaches and owners, and sometimes even by players. This practice continued until Ben Kerner, the owner of the St. Louis Hawks, explained to his colleagues that their condemnation of the officials was counterproductive.

In Kerner's words, "Knocking the officiating is like having the most expensive restaurant in town and then standing on the sidewalk in front of it yelling, 'My chef stinks!' "

The rest of the NBA owners saw the sense in Kerner's reasoning and instituted fines of up to $1,000 for owners, coaches, and players who publicly badmouthed the officials. These fines continue to be levied in today's NBA, with the stakes now much higher: The league can now assess fines up to $10,000 for this offense.

Back in the early days of basketball, the referees had to worry more about physical assault than mere verbal abuse. Around the turn of the century, there was only one referee; his prime concern was staying out of the way, for his own safety. The game was very rough, and the referee's standard uniform top, a white shirt, was frequently covered with blood when the game ended.

Spectators got involved by jabbing visiting players and referees with hat pins and lighted cigarettes. In the coal-mining towns of Pennsylvania, fans would bring nails to the game, heat them with mining lamps, and hurl them at the referee and at free throw shooters from the other team.

The most dangerous part of the game for the referee was the center jump, which at that time followed every basket. The two centers would usually collide with tremendous impact, and many a referee sustained serious injury when he did not clear out of the way in time.

If one team thought the ref was favoring the other, they came up with a way of dealing with it. As the ref tossed up the ball, two of their players would rush in from opposite directions and press the referee between them. That's right—this was the genesis of the basketball term, "the press."

Since the beginning of the game, basketball players have realized that the referees can greatly affect the outcome of the game. Naturally, players quickly sought ways to influence the judgment of the officials.

Back in the 1920s, the original Celtics came up with an effective technique. The first time a foul was called against them, all five of them would charge the referee, objecting strenuously to the call. Many a referee would then think twice before calling fouls against them.

There is no question that throughout the history of the NBA, several of its elite players have gotten away with more than their share of violations for most of their careers. In his book, *Second Wind,* Bill Russell claimed that all-time greats Bob Pettit and Oscar Robertson fell into that category. Russell claimed Pettit did not dribble very well and couldn't use his left hand much. But he somehow got the referees to let him take a few little steps before shooting, a break that enabled him to get off shots that he otherwise might not have been able to take. Once, during a game, when Russell protested that Pettit should be called for traveling, the referee answered, "Maybe he was walking, but he didn't go very far."

Robertson, according to Russell, was like a coach on the court, often completely taking over a game in the second half. "The Big O" enjoyed the benefit of what Russell called Oscar's Free Foul, when Oscar would dribble with one hand and fend off the man guarding him with his other arm.

Sometimes it takes the officials a while to learn a player's moves. When Dave

Cowens came into the league he was in constant foul trouble and fouled out fifteen times in his rookie season. But gradually the refs eased up on him, and his disqualifications were cut in half. Another highly touted rookie, Dave "Big Daddy" Lattin, was not that fortunate. After leading Texas Western to the NCAA title in 1967, Lattin took his board-crashing style of play to the San Francisco Warriors. He averaged one foul every three minutes and within two years was out of the league.

The NBA has now returned to a three-referee system, lessening the load on any one official. The referees can be thankful for that. And they also owe a debt of thanks to their most noted predecessor, Pat Kennedy.

Basketball's first famous referee, Kennedy made his mark in the 1930s when college basketball was developing a large nationwide following. Where most referees tried to avoid drawing attention to themselves, Pat was flamboyant. Fans thought he acted crazy, jumping and shouting while making a call and using a variety of sounds with his whistle—long loud blasts and short staccato toots.

Because Kennedy was a good referee, his flair was accepted and eventually imitated by other officials. In fact, his gestures evolved into the hand signals used by referees today. And, equally important, Kennedy was a man of unquestionable integrity who could not be intimidated. Consequently, he helped win new respect for the man in the striped shirt, the guy that everyone is trying to win over.

He Gave Up the Sport He Loved Best

If you remember the name Dick Groat, your recollection is undoubtedly of the hard-hitting shortstop who won the National League Most Valuable Player Award and the batting championship in 1960. Perhaps you remember him playing on World Series winners with the Pirates in 1960 and the Cardinals in 1964. Chances are you don't remember Groat playing his best sport, which was basketball.

Dick Groat began playing basketball at the age of five, when his brothers put up a basket in their backyard in Swissvale, Pennsylvania, near Pittsburgh. A fine all-around athlete, Groat chose Duke for his college education largely because of their strong baseball program. But while he was there, he developed into the best college basketball player in the country.

A 6′0″ guard, Groat was a great shooter and ballhandler, with a good change-of-pace move on his drive to the basket. He worked hard to improve his moves, receiving tips from Red Auerbach, who was an assistant coach at Duke between pro jobs. Groat had only average speed, but he rebounded well for his size. He was also a superb team player, and he was absolutely sensational in the clutch. In one widely heralded performance against Tulane in the Dixie Classic, Groat led his team from a 29-point halftime deficit to an incredible comeback victory, as he scored 32 of Duke's 74 points.

As a junior in 1951, Groat set an NCAA scoring record, averaging over 25 points a game. He also set a record for free throws in one season. As a senior, he again scored 25 points a game, and he also led the nation in assists. Groat was the only player in the country to make every All-America team, and was named College Basketball Player of the Year. Duke went 24–6, and more than anyone else, Dick Groat had glamorized college sports throughout the state of North Carolina.

Groat was featured in *Life* magazine twice in one year. One story was a pictorial feature of his matchup against Temple All-American Bill Mlkvy in basketball. The other was an article about the Duke baseball team, for whom Groat was also starring.

When the college basketball season ended in his senior year, his hometown team, the Pittsburgh Pirates, rushed him to the major leagues. Just three days after leaving the Duke campus, Groat played in his first big-league game. When the 1952 season ended, Groat's .284 batting average was the best on the team.

The Pirates agreed to let him play one year of pro basketball, and the Fort Wayne Pistons actually flew Dick to games on owner Fred Zollner's private plane, so that he could finish up his degree at Duke. Groat played well in the NBA, averaging 12 points a game and thrilling the fans with his ballhandling. But after 26 games, Groat was drafted into the army, ending his season, and ultimately his NBA career.

While in the service, Groat led his military base to worldwide army championships in baseball and basketball, the first time in history that the same base had won both. Groat intended to continue playing both sports when he returned home in 1955, but Pirates general manager Branch Rickey convinced him that his body could not take the punishment of playing close to 300 games a year as a starting shortstop and a starting guard.

Groat chose baseball, figuring it offered a longer career. His choice was a wise

Dick Groat might have been Hall of Fame material.

one, as he played until the age of thirty-six. But basketball was his first love, and in Groat's words, "If it was just a case of which one I like to play the best, it would be basketball. Just for fun, there's no other game in the world like it. In my opinion I was a 50% better basketball player than I was a baseball player. But Mr. Rickey was very persuasive."

Dick Groat had a long and outstanding career in baseball. But in basketball, he might have been Hall of Fame material.

The Two-Sport Champion

Former pitchers Ron Reed and Dave DeBusschere both played pro baseball and basketball for a few years. And Bo Jackson has now spent a couple of years playing baseball and football. But the only man since Jim Thorpe to have long-lasting success in two pro sports is Gene Conley, who played seventeen big league seasons—eleven in baseball and six in the NBA—in a span of eleven years. And Conley is the only man to win championship rings in both sports.

A 6′8″ center whose strength was rebounding and starting the fast break, Conley played behind Bill Russell on three of the Boston Celtics' championship teams from 1959 through 1961. Playing also as a backup forward, Conley averaged fifteen minutes a game in those years and was such a great leaper that he sometimes jumped center instead of Russell. But had it not been for an arm injury, Conley would never have been a member of those Celtics teams.

As a fun-loving rookie out of Washington State, Conley joined the Celtics in 1952 and laughed his way through the season, signing autographs as Celtics star Easy Ed Macauley. But on the court, Conley was all business, known for his rough rebounding style and a fierce competitiveness. A fine all-around athlete, Conley also signed with the Boston Braves, who felt he had a great future with them as a pitcher.

After one season in the NBA, Conley accepted the Braves' offer. They would allow him to begin the year in the major leagues if he would give up basketball. It appeared to be a wise decision, as Conley won fourteen games and finished third in the 1954 National League Rookie-of-the-Year balloting, ahead of a teammate named Hank Aaron. The next year, Gene was the winning pitcher in the All-Star Game as he struck out the side in the twelfth inning. But he injured his shoulder that year, and the arm continued to bother him for the rest of his career.

Despite taking frequent cortisone shots, Conley was still effective through the 1957 season, when the Braves won the World Series. But in 1958 he went 0–6 and was traded to the Phillies. Unsure of his pitching ability, Conley called Celtics coach Red Auerbach, who agreed to pay only for a one-way ticket to Boston so Conley could try out for his old job with the Celtics. Despite missing five NBA seasons Conley made the team, and the Celtics won the title. Conley pitched for the Phillies, too, and won 12 games for a last-place club. His dual career was underway, and it lasted five more years.

Gene Conley is often remembered for his escapades away from the playing surface. He was known to play with bad hangovers and often with no sleep. He became a legend in 1962, when he got off a Red Sox team bus in New York and disappeared for two days. He finally surfaced at a New York airport, waiting in line to buy a ticket to Israel—an attempt that was denied because he did not have a passport. Conley was fined $1,500 and had to promise to avoid alcohol. He finished the season with 15 wins on an eighth-place team.

Conley missed baseball spring training in those years. He would go right from the NBA playoffs to a Braves farm team for a few weeks. Conley often joked that he needed those weeks after basketball so he could get sufficiently out of shape to play baseball.

Gene Conley's career in both sports was a serious success. It has continued through his work in the NBA Old-Timers Association, which strives to get pension benefits for ex-players who played before the current pension plan existed.

High-School Basketball's Greatest Scorers

Some of the most impressive individual scoring explosions in high-school history are downright phenomenal. Wilt Chamberlain once scored 90 points for Overbrook High School in Philadelphia in 1955, and he didn't even play in the fourth quarter. In 1976, Billy Miller of Nancy, Kentucky, poured in 50 points, in one quarter. And a youngster named Walter Garrett accomplished something extra special in 1963.

Playing for West End High School in Birmingham, Alabama, Garrett scored every one of his team's points in a 97–54 win over Glenn Vocational. To keep Garrett from reaching 100, the opposition used all five of its players to guard him in the last few minutes. This was the final game of Garrett's high-school career, and his teammates deliberately missed their shots whenever they were unable to get him the ball.

Garrett fell far short of the schoolboy record for points in a game, though. That one belongs to Danny Heater, a guard from Burnsville, West Virginia, who scored 135 points on January 26, 1960 in a game against Widen, West Virginia. The *Wheeling Intelligencer* reported that the game was played in a small thirty-by-fifty-foot gym, with Heater trying to be sufficiently impressive to win a college scholarship.

The Burnsville team played a pressing defense against their inferior opponent, and fed the ball repeatedly to Heater. Danny scored 53 points in the first half and 82 in the second half, going 53 of 70 from the floor and 29 of 41 from the free throw line.

As it turned out Heater received that coveted scholarship, from the University of Richmond. But he was forced to drop out of college when his parents' home burned down, and he had to go to work full-time to help support them.

The high-school girls' one-game scoring record was set on February 24, 1924, by Marie Boyd of Lonaconing Central in Maryland. Playing under girls' rules, in which only a few players were allowed to shoot, Boyd scored 156 points as her team won 163–3.

Under current five-player rules, the record belongs to Cheryl Miller, of Riverside Poly in California. On January 26, 1982, Miller scored 105 points against Riverside Norte Vista. Miller, of course, went on to be an All-American at USC and led the US Olympic Team to a gold medal in 1984. And hers is probably the only name in this story familiar to any of today's basketball fans.

Cheryl Miller, a 100-plus scorer

Early Hazards of "The Cage Game"

In its early years, basketball was definitely a contact sport. Back in the 1890s, when the game was invented and quickly became popular, it bore many similarities to football. Basic equipment included elbow pads, knee guards, and even padded pants. There was only one referee, and most fouls went uncalled. Players threw elbows, shoulders, and hips, and broken noses were not uncommon.

The roughest part of the early game was the scramble for balls that went out of bounds, as players had to battle for the ball among spectators. Until 1902, whoever came up with the ball would throw it in, sometimes after a mad dash down a flight of steps at the corner of the gym. To keep the ball in play, large screens of chicken wire or rope were often used, giving the players the appearance of being inside a large cage. This led to the use of the term "cagers" to refer to basketball players, and to basketball's early nickname, the Cage Game. Often, players would get cut when thrown against the wire cage, a hazard that remained a part of the game well into the late 1920s.

Courts were small, making contact less avoidable than it is today, which led to some interesting strategy. Because the courts were usually just 40 feet by 60 feet, approximately half the size of today's courts, the walls were considered to be in play. Players caromed passes off walls, ceilings, pillars, and heating equipment. Often, a player would shake off his opponent by backing him into a hot stove or radiator at the end of the court.

Sometimes there were as many as a half a dozen pillars on the court; they could be used as picks into which you could run the man guarding you. Believe it or not, from this tactic came the term "post play," which we still use today.

Many of the gyms were so poorly lighted that players could barely see the basket. And many of the floors were also used for dances, and were so highly waxed that players would frequently slip and fall.

But there was one feature of the early courts that made possible a spectacular play. Since the end walls were in play until 1916, and the baskets were usually mounted on the wall, the man with the ball could literally run up the wall to lay the ball in the basket—the original version of today's slam dunk.

The NBA's First "Bird"

There has never been a stranger-looking NBA star than George Yardley, a 6′5″ forward who was bald, skinny, and knobby-kneed. But once this unusual specimen left the ground, he was clearly someone special. The NBA's best leaper in the 1950s, Yardley was the first pro hoopster with the ability to hang in the air and control his body before releasing a shot.

This move was almost unstoppable in those days, allowing Yardley to become the first man in NBA history to score 2,000 points in one season. He achieved that feat with the Pistons in 1957–58, averaging 27.8 points a game for a team that went 33–39. The Pistons did possess a fine playmaking guard in Dick

The first "Bird," George Yardley

McGuire, who finished second in the league in assists after feeding Yardley all year. But surpassing the 2,000-point plateau did not come without a real struggle.

In the last game of the season, Yardley needed 25 points as the Pistons were playing the Syracuse Nationals, whose coach, Paul Seymour, had vowed to hold Yardley under 2,000. He assigned defensive ace Al Bianchi to guard Yardley, a move that proved futile when Yardley pumped in 13 points in the first quarter. In the second half, when Yardley's total had reached 1,998, the Nationals triple-teamed him and denied him the ball for ten straight minutes. But Yardley finally broke ahead of the field on a fast break and dunked to reach the magic 2,000.

Yardley was known to his teammates as "Bird," which was commonly thought to be in recognition of his ability to soar above his opponents. Actually, the nickname was given to him by his college fraternity brothers, who once forced him to do menial tasks like those soldiers called Yardbirds in the army. The name Yardley became Yardbird, and then just "Bird." But it was a nickname that NBA fans almost never got a chance to know.

George was a civil engineering major in college at Stanford, and he didn't intend to play in the NBA. He was an All-American in volleyball and a great tennis player, but his basketball career was unspectacular. He passed up the NBA for three years after college, playing AAU ball while hoping to play in the 1952 Olympics. But a broken hand suffered just before the Olympic trials ended that dream, and when he finished military service in 1953, he was willing to talk with the Pistons.

Yardley had his engineering degree to fall back on, and he held out for $9,500, staying in shape in the meantime by playing volleyball. He almost quit after a mediocre rookie year, but he doubled his scoring average to 17 points a game the next season. The Bird was on his way.

Yardley played only seven years in the NBA, but his team made the playoffs every year. He retired to a job in engineering at age thirty-one with a career average of 19.2 points. He'll forever be known as the league's first 2,000-point scorer, and the first "Bird" in the NBA.

The Short Life of the ABL

Not to be confused with the ABA (which eventually merged with the NBA or with the original American Basketball League back in the '20s, the ABL of the 1960s had little impact on the world of professional basketball. The league was found by Harlem Globetrotters owner Abe Saperstein, who was angry at the NBA owners because he had been denied a franchise in Los Angeles before Bob Short moved the Minneapolis Lakers there.

The eight-team NBA was doing well, and Saperstein felt that many other cities could support professional basketball. So he formed another eight-team league for the 1961–62 season, going head to head against the NBA only in Chicago and Los Angeles. The other ABL cities were Kansas City, Cleveland, Pittsburgh, San Francisco, Washington, and Honolulu. The league had little trouble attracting big names to be their coaches. Former NBA All-Star Bill Sharman coached the Los Angeles Jets, and he was joined in the coaching ranks by former NBA players Jack McMahon, Neil Johnston, and Andy Phillip, and by celebrated college coaches Phil Woolpert (University of San Francisco) and John McLendon (Tennessee State).

Attracting quality players was another matter. The NBA had everything going for it, most notably a proven record of stability, and the new league was unable to get more than a handful of NBA players to jump. Those few who did were not major stars. The most celebrated among them was guard Dick Barnett, who jumped from Syracuse of the NBA to Cleveland to rejoin his old college coach John McLendon.

Not only did NBA players ignore the new league; the top college stars were not interested either, other than using the ABL to coax more money out of the NBA teams that drafted them. The one exception was forward Bill Bridges of Kansas, who signed with Kansas City rather than with the St. Louis Hawks of the NBA.

Bridges led the league in rebounding and set the ABL one-game scoring record with 55 points. He also led the Kansas City Steers to the ABL finals, where they were beaten by the Cleveland Pipers. In the fifth and deciding game, Cleveland's Dick Barnett scored 26 points before a crowd of only 3,000. That was to be the ABL's only championship series, as the league failed to make it through its second season.

On December 31, 1962, commissioner Saperstein folded the league, admitting that not a single club was operating in the black. Saperstein declared the Kansas City Steers to be the second-year champions, as their 22–9 record was the best in the league. While that so-called championship has been long forgotten, the ABL did leave one lasting legacy: the 3-point shot, which was used in the league's entire season-and-a-half existence.

When the ABA was formed in 1967, they resurrected the 3-point shot, but it was in fact a creation of the ABL, a league that did very little else to distinguish itself.

UCLA's Record Winning Streak

In January 1971 UCLA was closing in on the University of San Francisco's NCAA record 60-game winning streak with 47 wins in a row. But the streak ended at South Bend, Indiana, when Austin Carr scored 46 points to lead Notre Dame to an 89–82 upset of the Bruins.

John Wooden's team was in between the Lew Alcindor and Bill Walton eras, and was led by All-American forward Sidney Wicks and guard Henry Bibby, with Steve Patterson at center. The Bruins immediately started another winning streak, and by the time they closed in again on the USF record, Wicks, Bibby, and Patterson had been replaced by the so-called Walton Gang, featuring Keith Wilkes, Larry Farmer, Greg Lee, and Larry Hollyfield along with Walton.

As luck would have it, Game #61, the potential record breaker, was scheduled for South Bend on January 28, 1973. Sure enough, the Bruins went in to the game having tied the USF record with 60 wins in a row. A capacity crowd of 12,000 jammed the Notre Dame Athletic and Convocation Center, fired up by a rally held an hour before the game, as Irish coach Digger Phelps looked for help from the "sixth man." A national television audience also awaited the game, which turned out to be far less dramatic than most people expected.

UCLA took to the same floor where they had last lost—exactly two years and five days after Austin Carr's offensive explosion had beaten them. But this time there were no heroics by the home team. Despite a deafening roar from the Irish fans, UCLA remained under control, as they snapped an early 8–8 tie and opened an 8-point lead after seven minutes.

At halftime the Bruins led 38–25, and the Irish never mounted a threat in the second half. Walton dominated both ends of the floor with 16 points, 15 rebounds and 10 blocked shots. The junior center was aided by 20 points from Wilkes and 16 by Farmer as the Bruins cruised to an 82–63 victory and a new

NCAA record of 61 consecutive wins.

The game's high scorer was Notre Dame forward John Shumate, who had 21 points and 12 rebounds. Shumate would prove to be an even bigger factor the next time UCLA came to town.

In his postgame remarks, coach Wooden said, "My players seem to relish winning here where it's a big challenge before this crowd." A big challenge indeed, as the Bruins found out again the following year.

Yes, after 88 consecutive wins, the streak ended on the same floor where the Bruins had last suffered a defeat three years before. This time, the Bruins were concerned that Walton might not be at his best, and perhaps would not play at all.

Bill Walton scored 32 as UCLA got its revenge.

Walton had hurt his back in a fall two weeks before, and he hadn't played in twelve days. But Walton suited up against the Irish and went on to play the full forty minutes.

With the big redhead hitting 12 out of 13 from the floor, UCLA built up a 9-point halftime lead, and they still led 70–59 with 3:32 to go. The Bruins appeared to have the game in hand when Phelps called what appeared to be a desperation time-out. Phelps called for his team to press, and that decision turned the game around. After the time-out, Shumate scored over Walton, then stole the inbounds pass to score again, cutting UCLA's lead to 70–63. The Bruins proceeded to turn the ball over the next three times they had it, with the Irish scoring a basket each time to make it 70–69. UCLA's Wilkes then drove to the hoop and was called for an offensive foul, the Bruins' fifth consecutive turnover. Lip-readers in the television audience could make out Wooden yell "You crook!" at the referee on that call.

With twenty-nine seconds left, the Irish intended to work the ball into Shumate, but he was too well covered, so it went to unheralded Dwight Clay, who fired a jumper from the right corner and fell into the crowd as he came down. The ball landed in the basket, and Notre Dame had a 71–70 lead.

Wooden called a time-out with twenty-one seconds left, plenty of time for the Bruins to set up a play. But Tommy Curtis missed a long shot and Dave Meyers missed on the tip-in. Notre Dame had the game in hand but lost the ball out of bounds with six seconds left. This time the Bruins got the ball to Walton, but he missed a twelve-foot jumper, and two Bruins missed shots off the offensive board as time ran out.

John Wooden makes his point.

The crowd was so stunned that it was a few seconds before they overflowed onto the court in celebration of their team's 71–70 victory. Shumate finished with 24 points and Irish guard Gary Brokaw had 25 as the Irish became the nation's number-one team. That lasted only one week, until a rematch was played at Pauley Pavilion in Los Angeles. This time UCLA demolished the Irish 94–75, with Walton pouring in 32 points.

The Irish had ended each of UCLA's last two winning streaks. And beating the Bruins was something that nobody else had done in over half a decade.

The Incredible Green Jumping Machine

Seldom has a nickname been as appropriate as that of "Jumpin'" Johnny Green, a man whose entire career was built on the incredible spring in his legs. And never has a player retained his leaping ability longer than Green did in fourteen NBA seasons.

A native of Dayton, Ohio, Green played little in high school, and served in the US Marines before going to college. Despite being only 6′5″, Jumpin' Johnny consistently out-jumped his taller opponents as he helped take Michigan State to a Big Ten title and a berth in the Final Four in 1957, his sophomore year. The Spartans won the conference again in 1959, when Green was the Big-Ten MVP, averaged 18.6 points, and set a Michigan State career rebounding record. People called him the human pogo stick, and it was easy to see why.

Although he was already twenty-five years old, Green was the Knicks' first-round draft choice as the sixth pick in the nation. New York coach Fuzzy Levane thought Jumpin' Johnny could be the best rebounder the Knicks had ever had, even though he would be going up against players as much as eight inches taller. Sure enough, Green did become one of the league's best rebounders, twice finishing among the top seven. He was especially good at triggering the fast break, and was content in his role without taking a lot of shots.

In fact, Jumpin' Johnny's outside shot was seldom seen. But that didn't prevent him from contributing on offense. He averaged 18 points a game for the Knicks in 1963, and he led the team in rebounds. But New York still lacked a legitimate center, and in 1965 they traded Green and two others to Baltimore for Walt Bellamy. Green's career began to suffer as his playing time decreased. He was taken by San Diego in the expansion draft of '67, then traded to Philadelphia and eventually released in training camp in 1969.

Green was thirty-five years old, but Cincinnati coach Bob Cousy thought he still had something left. Jumpin' Johnny joined the Royals for a tryout, and the results were nothing short of amazing. Cousy saw Green as "an inspirational player who can come off the bench and give a team a lift." But he became far more than that, as he played thirty minutes a game and averaged 15.6 points and 11 rebounds in his first year with the Royals. Cousy revitalized Green's career by giving him a major role in the Royals' running game.

The oldest player in the NBA at age thirty-seven, Green scored almost 17 points a game the following season and proclaimed it the best year of his career. For the second year in a row, his wise choice of shots earned him the league's best field goal percentage. With plenty of spring left in his legs, Jumpin' Johnny was still in there leaping when he injured a knee and underwent an operation in March 1973. Green worked hard to rehabilitate the knee, thinking that he had one good year left. But the Royals released him in training camp that year, and his career was finally over.

When he retired, Jumpin' Johnny had played fourteen years in the NBA, second only to Hal Greer. He was the third man in NBA history to play 1,000 games. And his high-flying style gave fans a taste of what would come later, when slam dunking became an art form.

The Hall-of-Famer Who Was Lost For $1,000

In 1948, there were two competing professional basketball leagues: the National Basketball League and the Basketball Association of America. Before the leagues merged the following year to become the NBA, the BAA teams controlled expenses by adopting a salary limit of $6,000 for first-year players.

This limit was severely tested in the spring of 1948 when the New York Knicks of the BAA were trying to sign 6′8″ Dolph Schayes, a local product who had starred at NYU and was already popular with fans at Madison Square Garden. Represented by his father, Schayes wanted more than $6,000 and was offered $7,000 by Syracuse of the NBL. Schayes would have preferred to stay in New York City, but Knicks owner Ned Irish refused to break the salary cap, and Schayes packed his bags for Syracuse.

That decision would haunt the Knicks for sixteen years. When the leagues merged the following year, Schayes and his Syracuse teammates became rivals of the Knicks in the NBA East—and Schayes became one of the greatest players in NBA history.

Schayes had been considered something special from the time he made the NYU varsity as a freshman at the age of sixteen. He was only twenty when he entered the pros, and he played until he was thirty-six with the Syracuse team that became the Philadelphia 76ers in his final year as a player.

A well-rounded player, Dolph was a rugged rebounder: he led the league in 1951 and finished his career in fourth place on the all-time chart. He had a great drive to the hoop and a deadly two-hand set shot, which helped him retire as the NBA's all-time leading scorer, an honor that he has since relinquished. He was also considered the best passer among the big men of his era.

But more than anything else, Schayes was known for his hustle and durability. He broke a wrist twice in his career but missed a total of only nine games. Both times, he played with a heavy plaster cast and adjusted his shot to account for it. For more than nine years he didn't miss a single game, and his streak of 706 consecutive games played is the third longest in NBA history.

A hard-working perfectionist, Schayes was a superb free throw shooter who led the league three times and was adept at drawing fouls. And in his fifteen full seasons with Syracuse, the Nationals never missed the playoffs.

Schayes led the Nats to the NBA title in 1955, one of six times he was named to the All-NBA first team. He also made the second team six times, and when he retired as an active player he coached the 76ers for three years, winning Coach of the Year honors in 1966.

Many NBA observers felt that had the Knicks signed Schayes, they would have dominated the league for years. That $1,000 decision altered forever the course of NBA history.

Dolph Schayes

A Case of Bad Timing

Although officially measured at 6′11½″, Ray Felix was considered one of the first seven-footers to play in the NBA. As such, he endured the cruel insults of fans who yelled "Freak!" and "Goon!" and other such names at him as he ran by. Their taunts were fueled in part by Felix's awkward style of running: as he made his way downcourt, his arms would flap in the air. He was also clumsy and would trip and fall from time to time.

Things didn't come easy to Ray Felix, a kind, sensitive man who was well liked by both his teammates and opponents. As a high-school player in Harlem, he had to squeeze into size-13 shoes, unable to find the size 15s that would have fit properly. Although he was sought by dozens of colleges and was recruited for UCLA by Jackie Robinson, he chose to attend Long Island University so he could remain in New York City.

That decision turned out to be a major mistake when the school was involved in the 1950 betting scandal. Although Felix had nothing to do with it, he lost his last two years of varsity play as LIU gave up basketball. Rather than transferring, Ray remained at LIU and earned his degree. He played in semi-pro leagues to stay sharp, and worked out hard, tossing a medicine ball to strengthen his hands and skipping rope to improve his agility. By the time his class graduated, he was NBA material.

In the 1953 draft, Felix was passed over by the hometown Knicks, who chose Walter Dukes instead. While Dukes made the Knicks look bad by signing with the Globetrotters, Felix made the Baltimore Bullets look great for making him their number-one pick. Ray won the Rookie of the Year Award, finishing fifth in the league in points (17.6) and fourth in rebounds (13.3). In the All-Star Game, he started for the East.

With the Bullets on the brink of folding the next year, Felix was traded to the Knicks, who hoped he would be the dominant big man they had long been without. But it didn't work out that way. The Knicks played a running game that Ray was not suited for, and his points and rebounds decreased in each of the next three years. The game seemed to pass Ray by. Never known for his agility (even his fans never called him Felix the Cat), Ray was not able to play away from the basket, where a center needed to play against the likes of the new breed of agile giants like Russell and Chamberlain. His limited mobility, poor ballhandling, and limited shooting range prevented him from playing effectively unless his team used a slow-paced, deliberate offense.

But he was still productive in the pivot, where his rebounding and shotblocking abilities were maximized. His intense desire to play and to win enabled him to play in 439 consecutive games over six seasons and led to several fights that earned him the nickname Fighting Felix. In one famous altercation, he decked Celtics tough guy Jim Loscutoff with one punch, but the normally mild-mannered Felix was embarrassed by his fistic prowess.

He preferred contributing in more conventional ways, and that he did after the Knicks traded him to the Lakers in 1960. Ray became a valuable role player and averaged over seventeen minutes a game when the Lakers made it to the NBA finals in 1962.

That was the last of his nine NBA seasons, during which he never made over $10,500. Felix arrived too early to ever make big money, and too late to take full advantage of his size and strengths. And his choice of LIU was yet another example of Ray Felix's ongoing case of bad timing.

John Havlicek of the Cleveland Browns?

John Havlicek came out of Ohio State in 1962 as a basketball All-American, but the big star on that great Buckeye team was not Havlicek, but center Jerry Lucas. Some pro scouts thought that Havlicek lacked the one-on-one skills to succeed in the pros. But Red Auerbach of the Celtics believed in

John Havlicek,
a former
NFL draftee

Havlicek, and drafted him with the final pick in the first round.

Some of those picked ahead of Havlicek turned out to be busts in the NBA, including the number-one pick, Billy McGill of Utah, who was taken by Chicago, and the number-three pick, Paul Hogue of Cincinnati, taken by the Knicks. Some went on to greatness, like Lucas and Dave DeBusschere. When it was time for the last pick in the first round, Auerbach considered going after forward Chet Walker of Bradley, but ultimately decided he wanted Havlicek.

Getting Hondo to Boston was not going to be easy. The Cleveland Pipers of the ABL (The American Basketball League) were offering more money than the Celtics. And though he hadn't played a down of football in college, Havlicek had been drafted in the seventh round by the Cleveland Browns of the NFL. Havlicek had been an all-state quarterback in Ohio high-school football, but the Browns saw him as a potential pass catcher.

Havlicek weighed the offers and ruled out the ABL because of his doubts about the league's future. Though the Celtics made an initial offer of $10,000, Hondo signed with the Browns—for $15,000 and an automobile.

Havlicek went to training camp with the Cleveland Browns in the summer of 1962 as a wide receiver, a challenging position for a man who had not played football in four years. And, although the Browns liked his sure hands, they used him in only one exhibition game. Hondo didn't catch a single pass before he was cut.

Although it didn't appear that Havlicek got a great chance to prove himself, it's hard to fault the Browns' decision; the man who beat him out, Gary Collins, became an NFL All-Pro. Havlicek headed for Boston, where he got plenty of opportunities with the Celtics.

As a rookie, Hondo averaged 14 points a game, playing primarily at forward. Eventually, of course, he became the best swingman in the history of the game. But had it not been for the talents of Gary Collins, Havlicek might never have played in the NBA. And although the Browns cut him early, they liked him enough to invite him back to their training camp in each of the next five years. But by then, he was unalterably attired in Celtics green.

The NBA's King of the One-Liners

Perhaps the most quotable player in NBA history, Johnny "Red" Kerr was also one of its steadiest and most reliable performers. For over eleven years he didn't miss a single game—a string of 844 consecutive games that remains the second longest ever in the NBA. And the streak would have been even longer had coach Paul Seymour of the Bullets not decided to stick with Jim Barnes and Bob Ferry up front in a game that the Bullets lost by 11 points to the Celtics on November 4, 1965.

At the time, the streak was the longest ever in the league, and Kerr's teammates were shocked and disappointed that he didn't get in the game. Seymour later claimed that Kerr had a twisted ankle, but Kerr says he was healthy. When asked what had motivated him to go eleven years without missing a game, Kerr replied, "I was afraid if I missed a game my wife might make me do the dishes."

Late in the streak, Kerr was chatting before a game with sportswriter Leonard Koppett of *The New York Times.* When Kerr ended the conversation, he said, "You'll have to excuse me while I go tell some more lies to my legs. I have to tell them, remember when I told you last night that this would be my last game? Well, I was lying. This, tonight, will be my last game."

Kerr played a total of twelve years in the league, eleven of them with the Syracuse team that later moved to Philadelphia. His departure came after the arrival of Wilt Chamberlain forced him into a backup role. Kerr asked to be traded, explaining, "When you play behind Wilt, all your future is behind you."

Never a big scorer, the 6′9″ center had a career scoring average of only 13.8, but he averaged 11 rebounds. His unselfish style of play featured some of the best picks ever set in the NBA. Kerr's real forte was his passing, and he often joked that his autobiography should be titled *Twelve Years in the Pivot Without the Ball.*

Kerr's career was remarkable in that he did not play basketball until late in his senior year of high school in Chicago. Johnny had always played soccer instead, the sport in which his father had starred in Scotland before coming to the United States. But young Kerr made the transition to basketball easily, and he attracted sixty scholarship offers. He chose the University of Illinois and led the Illini to the Final Four. Syracuse drafted him in the first round in 1954, and he helped the Nationals to the NBA title his rookie year.

After twelve years in which his team made the playoffs every year, Kerr called it quits as a player and was hired to coach the expansion Chicago Bulls. He won Coach-of-the-Year honors in 1966, when the first-year team won 33 games and lost 48—good enough to make the playoffs—as Kerr's sense of humor helped keep the team loose.

Big Red could probably have outplayed many of his players that year, but he knew it was time to retire as a player he said, when "I was driving the lane and was called for a three-second violation."

Now a broadcaster for the Bulls, Kerr still gets in his quips. Asked how he would have guarded Kareem Abdul-Jabbar, he replied, "I would've gotten up real close to him and breathed on his goggles."

The Greatest Free Throw Shooters of All Time

The NBA record for consecutive free throws belongs to Calvin Murphy of the Houston Rockets, who sank 78 in a row in a streak that stretched from December 27, 1980 to February 28, 1981. Only one other NBA player has ever made more than 63 free throws without a miss: Larry Bird sank 71 straight in 1990. But outside the ranks of organized professional basketball, there have been several shooters who make the NBA's best look like amateurs.

On February 28, 1975, a fellow named Ted St. Martin hit 1,074 consecutive free throws in a shooting exhibition. St. Martin, who made his living traveling around the country shooting free throws, obviously had a huge advantage over players who shoot their free throws in the midst of game competition. On June 25, 1977, St. Martin sank 2,036 straight free throws over a span of three days at a shopping mall in Jacksonville, Florida. He was then fifty-three years old.

Long before St. Martin came along, the premiere free throw shooter was Harold "Bunny" Levitt. On the night of April 6, 1935, at the Madison Street Armory in Chicago, Levitt began shooting at 7 p.m. and hit 499 in a row with his two-handed underhand shot. He then missed his 500th shot, but he went on to make another 371 without a miss. By then it was past midnight and the gym was almost empty, so Levitt called it quits.

Although he was only 5′4″, Levitt was later signed by the Harlem Globetrotters—but not to play for them. As a crowd-pleasing gimmick, they offered $1,000 to anyone who could outshoot him in a contest of 100 free throws. The prize was never collected, as Levitt never made fewer than 96 out of 100. The best of his opponents made only 86.

Even though Levitt's record of 499 in a row has been wiped out, it remains the best ever by a shooter using an underhand shot. But there are other "specialty" free throw records far more unusual than Levitt's.

What's more difficult than running off a long string of consecutive free throws? How about doing it while standing on one foot? Wilmer Hetzel of Melrose, Minnesota, once made 53 in a row while standing on his left foot. And just to show that he could go in both directions, he made 38 straight while standing on his

Calvin Murphy's mark still stands.

right foot.

Hetzel also sank 42 in a row with his left eye closed, and 18 straight with his right eye closed. But that's nothing compared to John T. Sebastian, who shot blindfolded on May 18, 1972, and hit 63 in a row. And, proving even bizarre records are made to be broken, Fred L. Newman shattered Sebastian's mark on February 5, 1978, when he made 88 shots, blindfolded, from the charity stripe without missing.

Newman's feat occurred at the Central YMCA in San Jose, California, a fitting site for such an achievement. For when basketball got started by James Naismith and his students at the YMCA in Springfield, Massachusetts, one player shot all of his team's free throws. Had that rule not been changed, men like St. Martin, Levitt, and Newman may have made it as more than just sideshow shooters: They might have been full-fledged NBA stars, the "designated shooters" of basketball.

The Biggest Upset in NBA Finals History

In April 1975 there appeared to be two dominant teams in the NBA—the defending champion Boston Celtics, led by John Havlicek and Dave Cowens, and the Washington Bullets, with their rebounding stars Wes Unseld and Elvin Hayes. Both teams won 60 games during the regular season, and no other team won even 50. But when the championship trophy was presented in May, accepting it was Al Attles, the coach of the Golden State Warriors.

The Bullets beat the Celtics in a 6-game Eastern Conference Final, while the Warriors needed the full 7 games to dispose of Chicago in the West. The Warriors had won only 48 games during the regular season and had only one star, 30-points-a-game man Rick Barry. No one else on their team averaged as much as 15 points a game. And they had no one approaching the dominance that Unseld and Hayes gave Washington on the boards.

In fact, the Warriors surprised everyone just by getting to the Finals. Before the season they had lost high-scoring forward Cazzie Russell to free agency, and they had traded veteran center Nate Thurmond. But Attles created a winning combination by using all twelve players, substituting almost like a hockey coach, inserting groups of players into the game together. Attles instilled the unselfish team attitude that had been his trademark as a player, and by using everyone, he got the most out of everyone.

Some of his players, like Rookie of the Year Keith Wilkes, were young, and many were fighting for their NBA lives. So were several of his recycled veterans. Attles's philosophy was, "When everybody plays, when everybody knows they're going to play, there is more incentive." Attles had ten different players average over ten minutes of playing time, which was unheard of. And his twelfth man, Steve Bracey, averaged eight minutes, which may never happen again.

The Bullets were heavily favored going into the Finals. Many predicted the biggest mismatch in NBA history, a one-sided 4-game sweep. They were correct in predicting the sweep. But they were wrong in thinking the Warriors would get swept.

In Game One, the Bullets opened a big lead, as expected. But the Warriors' bench erased it and Golden State came back to win. Game Two was the same story, as the Warriors' depth allowed them to overcome a big lead and win by a single point. In Game Three, there was no big lead to overcome as Barry had a hot night with 38 points. But again it was the Warriors' reserves—Phil Smith, Charles Dudley, Derrick Dickey, and George Johnson—who put the game away. The difference in bench points in the 3 games was staggering: Warriors 115, Bullets 53.

In Game Four at the Capital Center, the Bullets tried to keep a lid on Barry as Mike Riordan physically challenged him from the opening tip. Riordan was charged with 3 fouls in the first few minutes, and had a wrestling hold on Barry when Attles stormed off the Warrior bench to aid his star. Attles was ejected and had to watch the rest of the game on a small TV in the locker room. But he liked what he saw, as his team rallied from a 14-point deficit to get back in the game, fell behind by 8 late in the fourth quarter, and bounced back again to win 96–95.

Veteran guard Butch Beard sank the points that won it, and Rick Barry won the series MVP Award. But it was a team victory in the true sense of the word. The Bullets, despite their two giants, had been outrebounded by the swarming Warriors. As Unseld put it, "They simply played sounder, better basketball than we did."

The Warriors' success led to the eight- and nine-man rotations that most NBA teams use today. After all, Attles's strategy had led to the biggest upset ever in the NBA Finals.

Basketball's Best Pure Shooter

Born in Lebanon, Indiana, where his father had been a high-school star, Rick Mount began drawing big crowds to watch him shoot in elementary-school games. In high school he was a three-time All-American, and he was the first high-school boy to grace the cover of *Sports Illustrated*. "Rick the Rocket" was pursued by over 250 colleges, and even then many scouts felt that he was a better long-range shooter than anyone in the NBA except Jerry West.

The country's most heralded high-school player decided to stay in Indiana, enrolling at Purdue in 1966. In his hometown, folks put up signs reading, "Lebanon, Indiana . . . Home of Rick Mount." And fans at Purdue became equally excited, watching Mount pump in jump shots from 25 feet or more. Rick averaged 32 points, scoring 61 in one game, and made All-American three times, just as he had done in high school.

A slender 6′4″ guard, Mount catapulted the Boilermakers into the Final Four in his junior year (1969) with a last-second shot that beat Marquette. They lost in the Final to UCLA when Lew Alcindor scored 37 points and the Bruins held Mount to 8 points in the first half. Rick erupted in the second half to finish with

28, but by then the outcome was no longer in doubt.

After his senior year, Mount signed a $750,000 contract with the ABA Indiana Pacers, a major shot in the war with the rival NBA and one that eventually helped force a merger of the two leagues. While some NBA executives, including Boston's Red Auerbach, claimed that Mount was overrated, the ABA was overjoyed to have him. In the end, Auerbach was proven correct.

Rick was back home with the Pacers, playing his home games only twenty miles from his house. But he would have been better off somewhere else. Indiana coach Bob Leonard wanted an all-around guard who would make plays and play tough defense. But Mount, who had always been told to shoot whenever possible, did not have those skills. He had never become a good passer, and his defense suffered from a lack of quickness.

Three-time All-American Rick Mount

Rick played sparingly as a rookie, and when he averaged 14 points a game in his second year, a controversy raged over whether he should get more playing time. The Pacers settled the dispute by trading him to Dallas, who then shipped him to Kentucky. Then a rash of injuries set in, preventing Rick from ever playing a full season again. His first year with Kentucky was his best as a pro, as he averaged 15 points a game. But he was traded again the next year.

In 1974–75, his fifth pro season, Mount was finally putting it together, averaging 17 points a game with Memphis. But he separated his shoulder early in the year and missed the rest of the season. The next year, a severe hamstring pull cost him the entire season, as the team folded before he recovered. Then in September 1976 he tried to come back with the hometown Pacers, but he quit in training camp. He announced that he had lost his desire and was tired of all the traveling.

Rick went back home and bought a sporting goods store in Lebanon, where his son continued the family tradition of starring on the high-school basketball court. Looking back on his five-year pro career, Rick regrets signing with the Pacers, saying, "If I had it to do over, I'd go to the NBA. Signing with Indiana was the worst thing I ever did."

Despite his failure as a pro, Mount is still considered by many to be the best pure jump shooter ever to play the game.

The Courtship of Moses Malone

Many of the stories in this book tell of talented high-school players recruited by dozens of colleges offering scholarships and much, much more. But none of them generated the attention received by young Moses Malone of Petersburg, Virginia, in 1974. Already 6′11″, Malone averaged 35.8 points, 25 rebounds, and 12 blocked shots as a high-school senior. His team won the state title for the second straight year and ran up fifty wins in a row.

College recruiters flooded the small Malone home, forcing Moses, a withdrawn young man, into periods of hiding. Most of his mail remained unopened, and when the doorbell rang, Moses often concealed his giant body underneath his bed. One coach from New Mexico lived in a Petersburg motel for two months. And Malone later said that eight or ten schools made offers that were illegal.

Washington State coach George Raveling expressed the feeling of everyone when he said, "Moses will rewrite the Ten Commandments of basketball." Reportedly, Oral Roberts himself visited Malone's mother Mary and told her he would heal her ulcers if Moses attended Oral Roberts University.

Mary had raised Moses by herself since the boy was two years old, and was working as a meat wrapper in a grocery store for $100 a week. She hadn't led an easy life, but it would certainly improve if she and Moses made the right decisions.

Somehow Maryland coach Lefty Driesell was the most persuasive; in June, Moses signed a letter of intent with the University of Maryland. Within two

Moses Malone disappointed Maryland fans.

months, the Terrapins had sold out their home games at Cole Fieldhouse for the entire season. But those eager fans never got to see Malone in a Maryland uniform.

The Utah Stars of the ABA had drafted Malone in the third round of their draft, but they made no immediate effort to sign him. Then, just before Malone was to begin classes, the Stars' new owner Jim Collier made Malone an offer, and Moses turned to attorney Donald Dell to represent him. Driesell tried desperately to convince Malone to honor his commitment to Maryland, explaining that if he played one year at Maryland, he could apply for the NBA hardship draft. But Utah's money was there for the taking, and Malone could not turn down a multiyear contract that guaranteed him a reported $1.28 million plus incentives.

While many college coaches denounced his decision, Malone's explanation was simple and sensible. "I gotta take care of my Momma," he said. According to a story in *Sports Illustrated,* Malone also told Dell that his hero had been Spencer Haywood, who turned pro after just one year in college. Moses claimed that at the age of fourteen, he had resolved to outdo Haywood's accomplishment.

Many outspoken experts, including Celtics coach Tommy Heinsohn, doubted that Malone was ready for pro basketball. But others, including NBA scout Marty Blake, disagreed. And, in his first pro game, Malone proved the latter group to be correct. Starting at forward against Julius Erving and the Nets, Malone scored 19 points and had 11 rebounds. Only nineteen years old, Malone was asked after the game about the difference between high school and the pros. He replied, "In high school you are younger. In the pros, you are older."

Meanwhile, on the Maryland campus, the hottest selling item was a T-shirt which bore the inscription "Moses Who?"

Kansas' Biggest Catch

When seven-foot center Wilt Chamberlain left Overbrook High School in Philadelphia, he selected Kansas from over two hundred colleges that had recruited him. Legendary Jayhawk coach Phog Allen, who was about to close out his long career, jubilantly predicted, "With him, we'll never lose a game. We could win the national championship with him, two sorority girls, and two Phi Beta Kappas." But at the age of seventy Allen was forced to step down in 1956, the year Chamberlain was to begin his varsity career.

Under new coach Dick Harp, who had been Allen's assistant, Wilt led the Jayhawks to the Big Eight title in his sophomore year, losing only once (to Iowa State) during the season. Chamberlain averaged 30 points and 16 rebounds, despite special defenses and stalling tactics designed to stop him.

The second-ranked Jayhawks breezed into the Final Four in 1957 and destroyed defending champion San Francisco in the semifinals, setting up a championship showdown with North Carolina. Although the Tar Heels were undefeated and ranked number one, their All-American center Lennie Rosenbluth was only 6′5″, and with the game being played in Kansas City, most fans expected the hometown Jayhawks to prevail.

In the title game, North Carolina coach Frank McGuire employed the same strategy that Iowa State had used in beating Kansas, featuring a 2-1-2 zone with their center always on Chamberlain and the two forwards coming in from the sides to help keep Wilt away from the boards. Offensively the Tar Heels were very deliberate, taking only high-percentage shots, and then only if Wilt was nowhere near the shooter.

Hitting 65% of their shots, the Tar Heels took a 29–22 halftime lead, as Kansas refused to take the open corner shots allowed by the North Carolina defense. But Kansas sped up the pace in the second half and led 40–37, with ten minutes left. The Tar Heels, who had played a triple-overtime game against Michigan State the previous night, appeared exhausted, and three of their starters were in foul trouble. But Kansas decided to freeze the ball, holding it for five minutes, which allowed the Tar Heels to catch their breath.

The final few minutes featured two lead changes and two brief skirmishes. During one, Chamberlain and Pete Brennan began wrestling. McGuire came off the North Carolina bench and got punched in the stomach before order was restored. The second half finally ended in a 46–46 tie, causing the first overtime ever in a national title game. With Rosenbluth having fouled out, the Tar Heels used a freeze in the overtime, and Kansas followed suit. Each team scored only 2 points in the first overtime; in the second overtime, *no one* scored.

With six seconds left in the third overtime, Jack Quigg hit two free throws to give North Carolina a 53–52 lead. When Kansas tried to force the ball into Chamberlain, Quigg intercepted the pass to seal the victory. The Tar Heels had won, despite Chamberlain's game-high 23 points.

The next year, teams played Wilt even tougher. Although his average increased, Kansas lost the Big Eight title to Kansas State, went 18–5, and failed to make it to the Final Four. A frustrated Chamberlain quit, claiming that opposition strategy ruined the game. He pointed out that Oklahoma State once passed the ball 160 times before taking a shot. Wilt joined the Harlem Globetrotters for what would have been his senior year, leaving both Chamberlain and Phog Allen's prophecy sadly unfulfilled.

The Toughest Player Ever

One of the best defensive guards in basketball history, Al Attles checked in at only 6′1″ and 175 pounds, but he did a superb job containing the opposition's highest-scoring guards. One of them, Lenny Wilkens, once said, "Al wasn't dirty, but he was on you like a glove all the time."

Attles played eleven years with the Warriors, despite the fact that he was a poor shooter and averaged only 11 points a game. But he got more than his share of loose balls, never hurt his team by taking bad shots, and was good at getting the ball quickly upcourt. And he was absolutely without equal in the rougher aspects of the game.

Attles looked menacing on the court, and despite his size, played the role of team enforcer. He was nicknamed "the Destroyer" for his ability to fight off picks—and just plain fight. Teammate Tom Meschery, a tough guy himself, called Attles "the toughest single fighter I ever saw in the league." Attles once saved Meschery from bodily harm by containing an enraged 6′8″, 250-pound Wayne Embry, who was trying to get at Meschery. Several of his fights against much larger opponents became legendary.

In the '60s, Al Attles's era, there were only nine teams in the league, creating deeper rivalries and actual feuds, and fighting was tolerated far more than it is today. In one game, 6′9″ Zelmo Beaty of St. Louis punched Meschery under the basket. Attles came charging from the free throw line to defend his teammate, lowered a shoulder, and sent Beaty soaring into the courtside seats. Attles and

Beaty then brawled amid the terrified spectators.

His most memorable encounter came in 1963 at Madison Square Garden against 6′8″ Bob Ferry of the Pistons. The two players collided chasing a loose ball, whereupon Attles threw Ferry over his head and jumped on him. As players from both sides joined in, Attles pummeled Ferry mercilessly. Warrior center Wilt Chamberlain moved into the fray, tossed Bailey Howell of the Pistons across the court and dumped seven-foot Walter Dukes into the courtside seats on his way to Attles. The 6′6″ Detroit assistant coach Earl Lloyd was trying to pull Attles off, without success, when Chamberlain arrived and pried Attles away by picking him up and carrying him off.

As Wilt explained later, "I had to get my boy Al before he killed Ferry." The fight, which lasted over a minute, caused Attles's ejection from the game. As he left the court, he was reprimanded by his mother, who had come over from New Jersey to watch the NBA doubleheader. Al's mom gave him a much harder time than Ferry did, putting the finishing touches on one of the NBA's legendary incidents. Ferry later said that Attles hadn't hurt him. Chances are, he'd been too dazed to remember.

Attles's reputation was well known around the league, but every now and then he was tested. Once, when a rookie played dirty against Al one time too often, Attles decked the kid with one punch. Before the rookie could get to his feet, the

Al Attles played the enforcer role.

referee stepped on top of him and advised, "Stay down, or it may be the last time you get up."

With the harsh penalties handed out for fighting in the NBA today, Al Attles will undoubtedly retain his title as the roughest customer who ever put on an NBA uniform.

The NBA's All-Time Iron Man

One of the greatest athletes ever to play in the NBA, Randy Smith went from high school in Bellport, New York, to Buffalo State University as a highly recruited track star. The school's basketball coach was unaware that he even played the sport. But Smith soon was excelling as a 6′3″ forward, in addition to high jumping and triple jumping on the track team. In his spare time, he managed to win All-America honors in soccer.

When the Buffalo Braves used a seventh-round pick to draft Smith in 1971, it was thought to be a public relations move, and Braves general manager Eddie Donovan later admitted that he never expected Smith to make the team. But coach Dolph Schayes was so impressed by Randy's speed that he kept him as his twelfth man. By the end of his rookie season, Smith had worked his way up to a starting guard position.

The fastest player in the league, Smith used his speed to great advantage, pressing on defense and wearing down opposing defenders who had to chase him around the court. He ranked among the league leaders in steals many times, and his high-jumping ability made him a good rebounder and spectacular dunker. Smith was a truly amazing physical specimen, once described by Braves trainer Ray Melchiorre as having "legs like Secretariat. You could take him into an anatomy class and show them every muscle in his body."

Smith was the MVP of the 1978 NBA All-Star Game, in which he scored 27 points. But his name lives on primarily because of his durability. From February 18, 1972, through March 13, 1983, Smith went over eleven years without missing a game—a streak of 906 consecutive games that remains the NBA record. It almost ended several times, once because of a hip injury and another time because of a serious case of the flu that he shook off sufficiently to score a career-high 41 points. When his wife was having their baby in 1980, he wanted to leave the team to be with her. "You take care of the streak," she said. "I'll take care of the baby."

As he closed in on Johnny Kerr's NBA record of 844 straight games, Smith had a more serious scare. He was released by the Knicks after the 1982 season, and had no job that fall, with his streak just 3 games shy of Kerr's record. But twenty-four hours before their opening game, the San Diego Clippers suddenly needed a guard. Smith was living in San Diego, and when located by coach Paul Silas, agreed to suit up and play. Smith scored 13 points and won himself a job, and the streak remained intact.

Several days later, Smith broke the record in Philadelphia, where Kerr, in a pregame ceremony, officially passed on the nickname Iron Man to Smith. The streak finally ended later that season, but not because Smith was incapable of playing. On the contrary, the thirty-four-year-old guard was averaging close to 10 points a game and was perfectly healthy. But he asked to be placed on waivers, hoping to be picked up by a playoff contender. Technically he was still San Diego property when they played a game without him, ending the streak.

Smith was picked up by Atlanta, but they were knocked out in the first round of the playoffs, and he never played another game in the NBA. But the chance at an NBA title, something that had eluded Randy his entire career, was worth giving up his private goal of playing 1,000 consecutive games.

The Iron Man

The NBA's Unrecognized Iron Man

While Randy Smith's streak of 906 consecutive games played is the official NBA record, pro basketball's longest streak actually belongs to Ron Boone, who never missed a game in his 1,041-game career. But since over half of those games were played in the ABA, Boone's achievement remains unrecognized in the NBA record book.

That may be the only place where Boone is not regarded as the game's all-time endurance champion. Ron says that he never missed a game in his life, dating back to the fourth grade in Omaha, Nebraska, when he first picked up a basketball. At Idaho State, Ron averaged 20 points a game, but at 6′2″ he was not considered a prime prospect. Drafted in the eighth round of the 1968 ABA draft by the Dallas Chaparrals, and in the eleventh round of the NBA draft by Phoenix, Boone signed with Dallas for $15,000. He spent his first 2½ pro seasons with the Chaparrals before being traded to Utah in 1971.

Boone was a fine all-around guard who excelled on defense and had a good outside shot. He led the Stars to the ABA title that year, prompting general manager Vince Boryla to say that getting Boone was "the best trade I ever made." And Stars coach Bill Sharman said, "Getting Ron was what won us the championship. Ron was so tough in the playoffs I always called him 'the Al Attles of the NBA.'"

Toughness was Boone's trademark, and his all-out physical style of play made his streak even more incredible. A fanatic about staying in shape year-round, Boone avoided serious injuries, never took a painkiller, and never made a token appearance just to keep the streak intact. Twice he remained in the lineup despite a separated shoulder. In one of those periods, he had to dribble exclusively left-handed because his right hand was badly infected from a fight two nights earlier. And, in 1978, he played for weeks with a face mask to protect a broken nose.

Boone endured all sorts of hardships in his eight years in the ABA, not the least of which was having to slide across the ice-hockey rink to get to the court at the Long Island Arena, where the Nets used to play. But Ron was very well organized and felt that getting lots of sleep was a key to his durability. While on the road, he would make the bed in his hotel room before leaving for a game so that he wouldn't have to return to a messy room.

When the leagues merged, Boone was selected by Kansas City in the dispersal draft. He was traded to the Lakers two years later, then to Utah, where he had won his only pro championship. The Jazz fans remembered his heroics with the ABA Stars, and when Boone played in his 1,000th consecutive game, he was named honorary mayor of Salt Lake City.

In January 1981 Boone was placed on waivers by the Jazz, the victim of a youth movement at the age of thirty-four. Until being waived, he had played in all 52 games that season, averaging close to 8 points a game. Boone went unclaimed, ending his streak at 1,041 games. It may not be an official NBA record, but in Sharman's opinion, "I think Ron's achievement is right up there with Lou Gehrig's."

And what does Boone think about those 662 ABA games not counting toward an NBA record? He gave his answer while the streak was still intact, saying, "If you put yourself out for 82 or 84 games a year for ten straight years, I don't see that it makes any difference what color the basketball is."

The Teams That Couldn't Shoot Straight

On May 30, 1988, the Detroit Pistons led the Boston Celtics 2 games to 1 in the NBA Eastern Conference Finals. In both of their wins, the Pistons had held the Celtics to 96 points or less. On this night, the Celtics would score only 79. Unbelievably, that would be enough to win, as the Pistons managed just

78 on their own home court at the Silverdome.

Great defense? To a certain extent, yes, but the uncommonly low score was created more by just plain bad shooting. It began with the lowest-scoring first quarter in playoff history, with the Celtics outscoring the Pistons 16–10. The Pistons actually led 8–4, then missed their next 20 shots in an incredible drought that lasted over ten minutes, stretching into the second quarter. Boston led at the half 46–36, but the Pistons had a big third quarter to take a 68–60 lead.

Incredibly, the Pistons then duplicated their pitiful 10-point first quarter with a 10-point fourth quarter that ultimately cost them the game. But they still had a chance to win it in the final minutes. With 1:18 remaining, Boston's Dennis Johnson sank an 18-foot jump shot to tie the score 78–78. Moments later, Detroit's Adrian Dantley tried to inbound the ball to John Salley with a lob pass designed to be an alley-oop. The ball floated beyond Salley's reach and went right into the basket. Because the ball was passed from out of bounds, the basket didn't count and was a turnover instead.

With eight seconds left, Johnson went to the free throw line to shoot two shots. He missed the first one but hit the second to give Boston a 79–78 lead. Detroit had the ball and one last chance. Not surprisingly, the game ended on a bad shot.

After a time-out, the Pistons got the ball in to center Bill Laimbeer, the game's high scorer with 29 points. Laimbeer had an open shot at the top of the key but passed it up and fed the ball to Joe Dumars, who lofted a jumper over the outstretched hands of Johnson. The shot was short, and Boston's Robert Parish grabbed the rebound in front of and above the rim to end the game.

The Pistons cried, "Goaltending!", but referee Ed Rush ruled that it was not goaltending because the shot had no chance to go in the basket. In that regard, it was no different than most of the shots taken that night.

The teams shot a miserable 36% from the field (Boston–40%, Detroit–33%) and their total of 157 points was the second lowest in playoff history. Back in 1956 the Fort Wayne Pistons had beaten Syracuse 74–71 in the only playoff game with fewer points.

Boston coach K. C. Jones called it "the weirdest game I've ever been in." Detroit coach Chuck Daly agreed. When informed of the shooting percentages, Boston's Kevin McHale pointed out, "A lot of those shots weren't even close. They were clangers and air balls."

The Pistons bounced back from this nightmare to win Games Five and Six and take the series before losing to the Lakers in the Championship Series. Somehow they survived one of the worst team offensive performances in NBA history.

The Only Woman to Try Out for the NBA

Ann Meyers grew up near San Diego as one of eleven children, and she got in the habit of competing against boys, including older brother Dave who went on to play in the NBA. She was good enough in high school to become the first woman ever to receive a full basketball scholarship from UCLA.

She made it pay off for the Bruins, leading the team in virtually every department as she became the first four-time All-American in women's basketball.

As a junior in 1978, she led UCLA to the national championship. In their 90–74 win over Maryland in the finals, Ann had 20 points, 10 rebounds, 8 steals and 9 assists—an impressive example of all-around play. Ann was known for her hustle and aggressiveness on both ends of the court, and she was respected more

After her UCLA career, Ann Meyers got a chance at the NBA.

for her passing and defense than for her shooting, although she averaged over 17 points a game in her college career.

At 5′9″ and 135 pounds, Meyers was an average-sized women's basketball player and appeared headed for the new Women's Basketball League after leaving UCLA. Instead, the world of sports was shocked to learn that Annie had signed with the Indiana Pacers of the NBA. In an unprecedented arrangement, the Pacers' new owner Sam Nassi gave Meyers a guaranteed contract for $50,000. If she failed to make the team, she would earn the salary as a commentator on Pacers telecasts.

Nassi denied accusations that the signing was a publicity stunt, and Meyers insisted she could compete with men, having played in pickup games at UCLA against college and NBA players. "I can dribble and make plays as well as anyone in the league," she said. "I don't want to embarrass anyone, including myself."

But only two NBA players at that time were as short as Meyers: Calvin Murphy and Charlie Criss. And they each outweighed her by thirty pounds, were tremendous leapers, and were much faster and stronger than Ann. Criss sent her an encouraging telegram and stated, "Ann Meyers must be some kind of lady. More power to her." But few thought that Ann could survive long in a league whose average player stood 6′6″ and weighed 205 pounds.

The Meyers signing outraged people around the NBA. Boston's Red Auerbach spoke for most of them when he said, "Annie's a nice girl but this is reminiscent of Bill Veeck signing that midget." While two other women had been drafted by NBA teams, Denise Long in 1969 and Lusia Harris in 1977, neither one had ever signed.

When Meyers reported to the Pacers' rookie camp, general manager-coach Bob Leonard, who had not been consulted before the Meyers signing, insisted, "She's just another athlete to me." But no other player in camp was flooded by requests for interviews with *Time, Newsweek, People, Wide World of Sports,* and *The Today Show.*

Ann battled until the end of rookie camp, when she was cut by Leonard, who commented, "From a fundamentals standpoint, Ann is excellent. Some of the guys had better thank God that she doesn't have about six more inches and forty more pounds." The disappointed Meyers had no regrets, saying, "It's something I'll cherish for the rest of my life. It was the chance of a lifetime, to be the first at something."

Meyers spent 2½ months on the Pacers broadcast team, then left to join the New Jersey Gems of the Women's Basketball League, where she was twice selected as the league's MVP. While some maintain that's where she should have been all along, Pacers assistant coach Jack McCloskey appreciated Meyers' efforts in Indiana. He recalled that after being cut, "She gave me a little peck on the cheek and a hug. It meant a lot to me. I've never gotten a kiss from a player who got cut."

Now married to Baseball Hall-of-Famer Don Drysdale and the mother of two children, Ann remains the only woman ever to sign with an NBA team.

Baseball or Basketball?

In the mid-60s, the Detroit Pistons had two forwards who had to choose between careers in baseball and basketball. While Dave DeBusschere went on to greatness in basketball, Ron Reed chose the other path. But he too made the right choice.

Born in La Porte, Indiana, in the heart of basketball country, Reed attended Notre Dame, where he broke the university's single-season scoring record with an average of 20 points a game. A 6′6″ forward, Reed was drafted by the Pistons in the third round of the 1965 draft, but he also received a tryout as a pitcher with the Milwaukee Braves. Reed had been a better basketball player than baseball player in college, and preferring basketball, he signed with Detroit.

As a rookie with the Pistons, Reed averaged 7.5 points, coming off the bench to play about seventeen minutes a game. The next year, he was the team's sixth man until late in the season when the Pistons acquired Wayne Hightower. Reed was averaging 8.5 points a game but playing less and less. Then, on February 15, 1967, DeBusschere, the Pistons' player-coach, became ill early in the game and removed himself from the lineup. Reed replaced him and scored 22 points.

Was this the turnaround point in Reed's basketball career? On the contrary. After the game, Reed marched into DeBusschere's office and announced that he was quitting basketball immediately to sign a two-year contract with the Braves. It was time for spring training to start, and the Braves had promised Reed a chance to make the big-league team if he reported to Florida on time.

Reed explained his decision, saying, "I didn't want the life of a bench-warmer, so I turned to baseball. I had been playing terrible basketball this year. I don't think I've been helping the team. I want to play a sport where I can help the team. I hope it's baseball."

DeBusschere, who had made the opposite choice just eighteen months earlier, had mixed emotions. While sympathetic to Reed's situation, he complained, "Reed was to be with us until the end of the season. We needed him fighting for the playoffs and he had signed a contract."

The Pistons failed to make the playoffs and Reed failed to make the Braves that year. But Ron made the big leagues in 1968, and the next year he won eighteen games as he helped pitch the Braves to a division title. A fierce competitor who once almost slugged it out with a manager who pulled him from a game, Reed went on to pitch nineteen years in the majors, playing for six division champions and two World Series teams.

Used both as a starter and in relief, he won 146 games and added 103 saves, one of just a handful of pitchers who have hit the century mark in both wins and saves. Looking back on his brief NBA career, Reed had no regrets. "I didn't have the talent for it," he insisted. "I knew I had no chance for any longevity."

Reed certainly achieved the longevity on the mound that he felt would have been impossible on the court. One final note: Reed's last two NBA points came on a dunk against Wilt Chamberlain, a memory that no doubt survived over 750 big-league baseball games.

The NBL, the BAA and the NBA

The Basketball Association of America (BAA) got started in 1946, when college basketball was booming at the box office. The existing pro league, the National Basketball League, was based almost entirely in the Midwest. The major Eastern cities were not represented in a professional basketball league, and the BAA was created to fill that void.

The new league had eleven teams, many of which were ignored by the public. One of the only gate attractions was the Philadelphia Warriors, who won the first championship. The Warriors were led by their high-flying star, "Jumpin'" Joe

George Mikan led the Lakers to the 1949–50 NBA title.

Fulks, the 6′6″ forward who is known as the father of the jump shot in pro ball. Fulks led the BAA in scoring with 23 points a game, including the then-phenomenal total of 41 in one game.

The average salary was about $5,000; Fulks received an estimated $15,000 as the league's headliner. Many players were paid by the game, and not very well. But most of the teams still lost money. By the start of the league's second season, four of the original teams had folded including Detroit, Cleveland, Toronto, and Pittsburgh. The BAA added a team in Baltimore and made it through the second year with eight teams. The circuit was clearly in trouble, though.

Competing with the National Basketball League for talent, the BAA decided to launch major player raids in the summer of 1948. Their strategy paid off. They successfully lured away four entire teams from the National Basketball League, including the Minneapolis Lakers, who featured the sport's hottest star, George Mikan. The 6′10″ center had just won his league's MVP award by receiving all 240 votes after leading the Lakers to the league championship.

As he had in the NBL, Mikan proceeded to lead the Lakers to the league championship and to lead the league in scoring. Averaging 28 points a game, Mikan drew huge crowds wherever he went, and when the Lakers played in New York, the Garden marquee would read, "Knicks against George Mikan."

The loss of Mikan and four teams doomed the NBL. They struggled through one more season, after which the survivors were taken in by the BAA. The unified league was renamed the National Basketball Association, or the NBA. The new league began 1949 with seventeen teams.

The seventeen teams were divided into three divisions under some awkward

1949–50 NBA STANDINGS

	W	L	Pct.	Games Back
Eastern Division				
Syracuse	51	13	.797	...
New York	40	28	.588	13
Washington	32	26	.471	21
Philadelphia	26	42	.382	27
Baltimore	25	43	.368	28
Boston	22	46	.324	31
	W	**L**	**Pct.**	**Games Back**
Central Division				
Minneapolis	51	17	.750	...
Rochester	51	17	.750	...
Fort Wayne	40	28	.588	11
Chicago	40	28	.588	11
St. Louis	26	42	.382	25
	W	**L**	**Pct.**	**Games Back**
Western Division				
Indianapolis	39	25	.609	...
Anderson	37	27	.578	2
Tri-Cities	29	35	.453	10
Sheboygan	22	40	.355	16
Waterloo	19	43	.306	19
Denver	11	51	.177	27

conditions, as the teams from the BAA did not want to play many games against the teams from the NBL, who played in such small-time locales as Sheboygan, Wisconsin, and Waterloo, Iowa.

As a result, some teams played as many as sixty-eight games, and others as few as sixty-two. The league's founders hoped that any inequities in the schedule would work themselves out in the playoffs, in which twelve teams participated. As many expected, no matter what sort of schedule was played, no team was going to beat Mikan and the Lakers.

In the regular season, the Lakers won their division as Mikan led the league in scoring with a 27-point average. Then, in the playoffs, Mikan averaged over 31 points a game as the Lakers won the championship by winning ten of their twelve games.

Although zone defenses were prohibited, few teams had their players drive to the basket or use the fast break, choosing instead to wait patiently for the good shot. Scores ranged from the 60s to the 90s, with only an occasional 100-point explosion. And while Mikan averaged 27 points to lead the league, only one other player, Alex Groza of Indianapolis, averaged over 20 points a game.

With the 24-second clock not yet in existence, teams with a lead in the fourth quarter would go into a stall, leading to some horribly boring games. Not surprisingly, six of the original seventeen teams—Chicago, St. Louis, Anderson, Sheboygan, Waterloo, and Denver—were not around for the NBA's second season. But stability was soon to come. The biggest boost for the NBA was the college basketball game-fixing scandal that broke the next year, souring many fans on the college game and turning them toward the pros. The NBA's future was assured.

1940–50 INDIVIDUAL SCORING LEADERS

	G.	FG	FT	Pts.	Avg.
George Mikan, Minneapolis	68	649	567	1865	27.4
Alex Groza, Indianapolis	64	521	454	1496	23.4
Frank Brian, Anderson	64	368	402	1138	17.8
Max Zaslofsky, Chicago	68	397	321	1115	16.4
Ed Macauley, St. Louis	67	351	379	1081	16.1
Dolph Schayes, Syracuse	64	348	276	1072	16.8
Carl Braun, New York	67	373	285	1031	15.4
Ken Sailors, Denver	57	329	329	987	17.3
Jim Pollard, Minneapolis	66	394	185	973	14.7
Fred Schaus, Ft. Wayne	68	351	270	972	14.3

The Little Man Who Made It Big

Perhaps you recall ABC's *Monday Night Football* announcers referring to their producer-director Chet Forte as a former college basketball player. But Forte was not just another basketball player before he began piling up Emmies. In fact, he was once the nation's College Player of the Year.

The son of a doctor in Hackensack, New Jersey, Fulvio Chester Forte Jr. entered Columbia University in 1953 as a pre-med major. It wasn't long before he rivaled his fellow Columbia student Pat Boone for national attention. Despite being only 5′9″ and 140 pounds, Forte was a scoring machine who freed himself to shoot with great fakes and drives to the basket. He was fast and deceptive, was deadly with a two-hand set shot, and could also hit the jumper.

In his first four varsity games, Forte averaged 31 points, causing opposing coaches to assign one man, usually a six-footer, to guard him, playing a zone with the other four men. Not even that strategy could contain Chet "the Jet," who went on to average 24.8 points a game in his varsity career, still the record at Columbia. Known for talking constantly to his opponents, Forte won the hearts of the fans, especially the shorter ones. And as a senior, he was up against college basketball's biggest man of all.

In 1957, Chet was battling 7′1″ Wilt Chamberlain of Kansas and 6′9″ Grady Wallace of South Carolina for the national scoring championship. Forte scored 45 points, a Columbia record, one night against Pennsylvania as part of his bid to win the title, but in the end, Wallace won it by averaging 31.2. Forte finished the season with an average of 28.9, but when the College Player of the Year votes were tallied, it was Forte on top. Even though Chamberlain led his team to the NCAA Final, he lost out to the man who was almost a foot and a half shorter than he was.

Before Forte arrived, Columbia's teams were usually mediocre. But in his three varsity seasons, they posted a record of 50–23, including 18–6 in 1957. Forte's value was never more evident than in the Orange Bowl Tournament in Miami, when he outscored All-American Hot Rod Hundley 34–28. Even though Columbia lost to West Virginia 70–60, Forte was named the tournament MVP.

Long before players wore their names on their jerseys, Forte was able to do so, with the number 40 on his back. Columbia's public address announcer, who usually announced a player's number and name when he scored, had to change his routine after a few too many calls of "Basket by number forty, Forte."

Among Forte's accomplishments was an NCAA record for consecutive free throws made (38), a mark that has since been broken. When his senior season ended, Forte became the first Ivy League player to sign a pro contract before graduation. But Chet was drafted into the military and never played a game of pro ball.

Instead, he joined ABC Sports in 1963 and won the first Emmy given for directing sports. He followed that up with many more during the seventeen years he directed *Monday Night Football*. It's a safe bet that few of his millions of viewers knew that they were watching the work of a man who had outplayed Wilt Chamberlain.

The Record-setting Dons

One of the greatest teams in college basketball history, the University of San Francisco Dons took the nation by surprise when they won their first national championship in 1955. In the preseason poll, not even one coach ranked them in the Top Ten. But in the next two years, the Dons won back-to-back national titles and compiled a record sixty-game winning streak.

The coach of this unexpected powerhouse, Phil Woolpert, had been hired away from neighboring St. Ignatius High School, where the Dons were forced to practice because there was no gym on campus. Since the Dons had to vacate the high-school gym by 3 p.m., and classes at USF lasted until one or two o'clock, Woolpert's team had less practice time than any other major college team in the country.

The stars of the team were two local products who had received scholarship offers from no school other than USF. One of them was a small guard who had been more serious about football than basketball at San Francisco's Commerce High. But Woolpert worked hard to turn him into a basketball star, a defensive wizard who could also score. The name of that unheralded 6′1″ backcourt man was K. C. Jones.

The other mystery sensation uncovered by Woolpert was a painfully sensitive 6′9″ sleeping giant who had not even made his high-school team in Oakland until his senior year, and who wondered if he would make the USF team even after receiving a scholarship. But this was the man who would revolutionize basketball with his shot blocking and rebounding. This, of course, was Bill Russell.

Along with Jones and Russell, the Dons featured 5′10″ guard Hal Perry, who gave them a third defensive standout. One forward, Stan Buchanan, was a fine all-around performer, and the other forward, Jerry Muller, was an outstanding shooter with a good hook shot. They also had a strong bench, which allowed them to play aggressive defense all night.

Entering their first championship season, the Dons were coming off a 14–7 record, but Jones had missed almost the entire year with a ruptured appendix. Even with K. C. healthy, they lost the third game of the '54–'55 season to UCLA. A distraught Russell openly wept in the locker room, claiming that the loss was his fault. That was the last time he would ever take responsibility for a San Francisco defeat.

After losing at UCLA, the Dons bounced back and beat the Bruins in a rematch a week later. With their confidence bolstered, they marched through the rest of the schedule without a loss. With defense their strong point, they advanced to the Final Four and beat Colorado 62–50, in the semifinals. In the championship game they faced defending champion La Salle, starring Tom Gola, the College Player of the Year. In a brilliant move, Woolpert assigned Jones to cover the much taller Gola, leaving Russell free to roam under the basket. The strategy worked, as Gola was held to 16 points. The Dons won, 77–63, with Russell winning the tournament MVP.

The next season was a cakewalk, as the Dons went undefeated, allowing only 49.5 points a game. They won by an average margin of 21 points, with their closest game a 33–24 win over a desperately stalling California team that once went eight minutes without taking a shot. They beat SMU by 20 in the NCAA semifinals and Iowa by 12 in the finals.

San Francisco had established a new NCAA record winning streak—fifty-five wins in a row. With Russell and Jones off to the NBA the next year, the Dons won their first 5 games to stretch the streak to 60, then lost at Illinois in a frosty gym with all the windows open. The shivering Dons hit only twenty-two percent from the floor, and lost 62–33. They recovered sufficiently to again make the Final Four, but lost to Kansas in the semifinals. That was the end of the USF glory years, but their 60-game win streak remained the record until broken by UCLA in 1973.

Backcourt defensive standout K.C. Jones

The NBA's "Shoeless Joe"

Nicknamed "the Nose," Alex Groza was the brother of Lou Groza, who went on to fame as an NFL placekicker. The two grew up in Martins Ferry, Ohio, which was also home to baseball's Niekro brothers and to John Havlicek. But Alex could have been the most successful of them all.

A powerful 6′7″ forward, Groza attended the University of Kentucky, where he was the big man on the 1948 team dubbed "The Fabulous Five." That team went 34–2 and won Kentucky's first national championship. Groza scored a team-high 14 points in their 58–42 win over Baylor in the Finals and was named the tournament MVP.

All five Kentucky starters won spots on the US Olympic team that won the gold medal that summer, so it was not surprising when they repeated as national champions in 1949. This time, the Wildcats beat Oklahoma A&M in the finals, 46–36, with Groza scoring 25 points. In three games, Groza scored a tournament record 82 points and was again named MVP. To top it off, he was also named College Player of the Year and earned All-America honors for the third year in a row.

Groza continued to shine when he joined the Indianapolis Olympians of the NBA. In only his fourth pro game, he burned the Knicks for 41 points before a crowd of 18,135, the largest ever to see a pro game at Madison Square Garden. Alex averaged 23.4 points that season, second only to George Mikan, and made the All-Star team.

As the two best big men in the league, Mikan and Groza had sensational duels each time they played, and their rivalry continued in Groza's second season. Alex again finished second to Mikan in scoring, averaging 21.7, and was a first-team All-Star again. But Alex Groza never played another NBA game.

On October 22, 1951, Groza and teammate Ralph Beard, who had also starred at Kentucky, were watching a preseason exhibition game at Chicago Stadium when they were arrested and brought to New York to face charges. Groza soon admitted that he and two Kentucky teammates had given less than their best effort in losing to Loyola in the NIT in 1949. Each player had received $500 for fixing the game, part of a widescale betting scandal that shook the basketball world.

Groza pleaded guilty and received a suspended sentence in exchange for cooperating in the investigation. But he was banned for life from the NBA. When he appealed to NBA owners for reinstatement, he was turned down unanimously, with even Indiana voting against allowing him to return. What appeared to be a certain Hall of Fame career was down the drain, and Groza turned to other vocations.

He worked for General Electric and as a sportscaster and helped out in his mother's tavern. Finally, in 1959 he was hired as basketball coach at little Bellarmine College in Louisville. He was the first person implicated in the betting scandal to return to college basketball in any capacity. Groza explained, "Finally I decided I couldn't hide anymore. I've done ten years of penance. People are really forgiving."

Groza coached at Bellarmine for seven years, then was hired as a scout by the ABA Kentucky Colonels. In 1970 he became the Colonels' business manager, and when the San Diego Conquistadors entered the ABA in 1972, they named Groza as their general manager. The team eventually folded, and Groza's basketball career was over. He went to work for Reynolds Metals in San Diego as a regional sales manager.

While he was ultimately successful in business, Groza might have been one of the greatest NBA players of all time.

The Most Damaging Punch in Basketball History

The most damaging punch in basketball history was thrown on December 9, 1977, in a game between the Lakers and the Houston Rockets at the Forum in Los Angeles. Early in the third quarter, seven-foot center Kevin Kunnert of the Rockets and 6′8″ Laker forward Kermit Washington collided under the boards. As the teams moved upcourt, the two men shoved each other and began fighting. Washington landed a punch that stunned Kunnert and left him holding the side of his face.

Meanwhile, 6′8″ forward Rudy Tomjanovich, the Rockets' captain and best player, raced back to help his teammate. As Rudy arrived on the scene, Washington whirled and landed a roundhouse right to the face that flattened Tomjanovich. Rudy dropped to the court unconscious, bleeding from the nose, mouth, and ears.

Referee Bob Rakel later said it sounded like someone had hit a concrete wall

Rudy Tomjanovich, after the punch

with a baseball bat. And while Houston coach Tom Nissalke called the blow "a sucker punch," Washington contended that he acted in self-defense, believing that Tomjanovich was leading a second wave of Houston attackers.

While Washington has always maintained that the punch was an honest mistake, the damage was unmistakable. Tomjanovich suffered a broken nose, a double fracture of the jaw, and a concussion, requiring three operations to rebuild his face. One of the surgeons said, "His face had to be rebuilt like a jigsaw puzzle." Rudy spent two weeks in the hospital, covering the mirrors with towels for several days so he would not have to see his own face.

Tomjanovich, who had been an All-Star four times in his eight years in the league, was lost for the rest of the season. At the time of the injury, he was averaging 22 points a game and was one of the league's premier power forwards. What happened to Kermit Washington?

Four days after throwing the tragic punch, Washington was fined $10,000 by NBA commissioner Larry O'Brien, the largest fine in sports history at that time. He was also suspended without pay for sixty days, which cost him an additional $50,000.

Tomjanovich sued the Lakers for failing to control the actions of Washington, who was known around the league as an "enforcer." The Rockets sued the Lakers for the loss of their captain, who missed 53 games. When the case came to trial in the summer of 1979, a federal court jury in Houston awarded Tomjanovich $3.3 million, which was even more than he asked for. The jury concluded that the Lakers had failed to adequately train and supervise their employee, and that Washington had acted with reckless disregard for the safety of others.

The Lakers appealed the ruling and eventually settled with Tomjanovich for an undisclosed sum. They also settled the lawsuit filed against them by the Rockets.

Tomjanovich was able to return to action ten months after the incident and played well, helping the Rockets make the playoffs. He retired as a player in 1981, with a career average of 17.4 points a game.

Tomjanovich says that he does not relive the incident, that there are no flashbacks since he never saw the punch coming. In many ways, the aftermath was tougher on Washington than it was on Tomjanovich.

At 6′8″ and 230 pounds, Washington was one of the strongest men in the NBA. But despite his reputation as one of the league's "enforcers," the Tomjanovich incident was the only fight he was ever involved in. In his five years in pro ball, he had fouled out of only four games, hardly what you would expect from an overly aggressive player.

In fact, Washington was popular with players around the league. An honors graduate in psychology from American University, Washington was sensitive and gentle off the court, a peaceful, caring man. In the words of Lakers general manager Bill Sharman, "Kermit is just the opposite of mean. He's almost timid away from basketball."

Yet it was Washington who unloaded the punch that he claimed was thrown in self-defense, "an honest, unfortunate mistake." It cost Tomjanovich 53 games and untold anguish. It cost Washington almost as much.

Kermit's fine and sixty-day suspension came at a time when he was having his best pro season, averaging 10 points and 9 rebounds a game as a role player off the Lakers bench. Washington received hate mail from all over the country, including racial slurs and death threats. He was hounded by crank telephone calls. All this, despite the fact that he constantly expressed his sorrow over the incident and made several attempts to contact Tomjanovich—calls that were never returned.

Three weeks into the suspension, Washington was traded by the Lakers to the Celtics, and when he returned to action, he was booed everywhere he played. Despite averaging 11 points and 10 rebounds with Boston, they traded him that summer to San Diego.

Ironically, his first game with the Clippers was against Houston, the first game for Tomjanovich since the injury. The two men guarded each other for an entire quarter without a handshake or a word spoken. They did discuss the altercation before a game two years after the incident, following the trial in which the Lakers had been found negligent for retaining a player with "a tendency for violence while playing basketball."

Washington was unable to shake that reputation for years. But this supposedly malicious player later devised what may have been the most compassionate undertaking in NBA history.

Late in his career, in 1983, Washington was attempting a comeback with the Portland Trail Blazers after injuries had limited him to just 20 games the previous year. In a stunning request, Washington asked the Trail Blazers for permission to anonymously give away his entire salary to fans who had fallen on hard times and needed the money to get back on their feet. Unfortunately, Washington's comeback attempt failed because of knee and back problems. But his program of assistance survived, with Trail Blazers players and management contributing.

Portland general manager Stu Inman said, "The world is going to be a better place because Kermit Washington walked through it." Unfortunately, one tragic moment kept most of America from ever knowing that.

The Jumper on the Run

The son of "Lefty" Flynn, a silent movie western hero who had been a football star at Yale, John "Bud" Palmer was destined to have an extraordinary life. Educated in Switzerland and at Phillips Exeter Academy, Palmer became one of the first athletes to become a successful sportscaster. He was an All-American in three sports at Princeton in the early '40s, starring in lacrosse and soccer as well as basketball. But it was on the basketball court that he made his most lasting impression, by helping to introduce the running jump shot.

Hank Luisetti of Stanford had already popularized the jump shot, but everyone seemed to be taking the shot from a stationary position. Palmer figured it would be a more dangerous weapon if he could shoot it on the run. Princeton coach

Cappy Capon thought the running jumper was too risky, and discouraged Palmer from using it, but Palmer became so accurate that before too long, Capon had little to complain about.

After graduating in 1944, Palmer spent a few years in the navy air corps then signed with the New York Knicks of the new Basketball Association of America. Despite joining the team in midseason, Bud led the Knicks in scoring, averaging 9.5 points a game. Knicks coach Neil Cohalan thought the running jumper was too unorthodox, and when Joe Lapchick took over as coach the next year, he agreed with Cohalan. But the shot kept going in, and Palmer made a believer out of Lapchick by finishing ninth in the league in scoring with an average of 13.5 points. (Remember, these were low-scoring times in pro basketball.)

A 6′4″ forward, Palmer was the Knicks' captain the following year, and again averaged over 12 points a game. But at the age of twenty-seven, in his basketball prime, Bud decided to retire to pursue a career in broadcasting and sports promotion. While playing for the Knicks, Palmer had done a television commercial, believed to be the first ever by a basketball player. His good looks and articulate speech made him a natural for the airwaves.

Palmer was an instant success on the air, beginning with color commentary and then play-by-play on Knicks games and college games at Madison Square Garden. Eventually, Bud worked for all three major networks, working events as diverse as football, golf, and the Olympics. And when CBS first televised a National Hockey League Game of the Week in 1956, Palmer became the country's first network hockey announcer.

In 1966, Palmer was appointed New York City Commissioner of Public Events, a job that made him the city's official greeter. Palmer hosted celebrities from around the world, moving in the loftiest of social circles. In 1972, he and his wife moved to Vail, Colorado, to escape the big-city rat race. And in 1976, he helped bring a National Hockey League team to Denver, becoming part owner of the Colorado Rockies.

Palmer had played hockey while living in Switzerland as a youngster, and he was committed to its success in Colorado. But this venture proved to be unsuccessful, as the team was ultimately sold and moved to New Jersey. It was one of the few failures for the man who helped proved that the jump shot could be effective—even while taken on the run.

The Man Who Made St. Louis a Basketball Town

Standing 6′8″ but weighing a lean 190 pounds, Ed Macauley lacked the power and strength that most great big men have possessed. But as a major force in the 1940 and '50s, it was "Easy Ed" who proved that a tall man could be successful with grace and agility rather than size and brute force. He could move, he could shoot, and he could handle the ball.

Born in St. Louis, Macauley attended St. Louis University and totally changed the nature of their basketball program. Before he arrived, the Billikens drew about four hundred fans a game to their campus gym. By the time he left in 1949, they were packing them in at the 11,000-seat Municipal Auditorium.

The son of an attorney, Macauley took his education seriously and did not play basketball his freshman year because a late class conflicted with practice. But he quickly made up for lost time; he was an All-American his last two years. As a junior, Macauley led his team to the NIT championship, which in those days was thought of as a national title. And, as a senior, Macauley had the pro scouts drooling as they watched his smooth style and stifling defense help his team go 22–4.

Macauley's family wanted him to pass up playing in the newly formed NBA, hoping he would instead join his father as an attorney. But Easy Ed had visions of putting St. Louis in the forefront of pro basketball. Macauley joined the St. Louis Bombers in 1949–50, the NBA's first season. But not even he could keep the team afloat. They finished last in their division, and folded at the end of the season. To get Macauley, the Knicks offered to buy the whole St. Louis franchise

Ed McCauley retired as a champion.

for $50,000. But the league would not allow it and awarded Macauley to the Boston Celtics, who had finished last in their division.

Macauley combined with Bob Cousy and Bill Sharman to make the Celtics one of the league's better teams. And, in the first NBA All-Star Game in 1951, Macauley was the high scorer with 20 points. Easy Ed starred for the Celtics until 1956, when the new team in St. Louis, the Hawks, brought him back home in the famous trade that gave the Celtics the right to draft Bill Russell.

In his first year back home, Macauley and the Hawks lost to the Celtics in the NBA finals. But the next year, the Hawks defeated Boston for the championship. Easy Ed decided to go out a champion and retired as an active player. He later served the Hawks as coach and general manager, and in 1960, at the age of thirty-two, he became the youngest man ever elected to the Basketball Hall of Fame.

As a pro, Macauley averaged around 18 points a game, handled the ball well, and played great defense. And as a sports hero in St. Louis, Easy Ed Macauley ranks right up there with the stars of the baseball and football Cardinals—one of the city's greats.

The Longest Championship Series Game in NBA History

The 1976 NBA championship series was tied at two games apiece, with the underdog Phoenix Suns giving the Boston Celtics all they could handle. Under coach John MacLeod, the Suns had barely made the playoffs with a late surge that enabled them to finish with a record of 42–40, while the Celtics had breezed to a division title with a 54–28 mark. Sparked by their two big scorers, Paul Westphal and Alvan Adams, and rebounding forward Garfield Heard, the Suns had made it to the Finals. After losing the first two games at Boston to Dave Cowens, Jo Jo White, and company, they won the next two games in Phoenix.

On Friday, June 4, a hot, muggy night, Game Five began at a steamy Boston Garden with the Celtics racing to a 32–12 lead. But the Suns battled back, and at the end of forty-eight minutes, the game was tied 95–95. Defense prevailed in the first overtime, leaving the teams tied at 101–101. In the second overtime the Celtics led by 3 points with fifteen seconds remaining. But Dick Van Arsdale scored for the Suns, and then Westphal stole the ball and fed Curtis Perry for the shot that put Phoenix up 110–109. The Celtics went to John Havlicek for the last shot, and he banked in a running one-hander to give the Celtics a 111–110 lead.

Hundreds of Celtics fans stormed the court, thinking that Boston had won, but one second remained. While order was being restored, Westphal shrewdly called a time-out, even though the Suns were out of them. This gave the Celtics a technical foul shot but allowed the Suns to throw the ball in at midcourt instead of from under their own basket. Jo Jo White hit the free throw to put Boston ahead by two points.

In the Garden mayhem, fans actually made their way into the Suns' huddle as the security forces were overwhelmed. But play finally resumed, and when it did, the Suns threw the ball in to Heard, who flung up a desperation rainbow-arced jump shot from the corner that miraculously swished through with the buzzer sounding. The teams would play a third overtime, the first and only time in championship series history.

The third overtime, played after midnight in Boston, was decided by an unlikely hero, as Celtics reserve Glenn McDonald hit the shot that gave Boston the lead for good. The Celtics won 128–126 in sixty-three minutes of playing time, and Heard set a championship series record by playing sixty-one of them.

After the game, one rowdy Celtics fan assaulted referee Richie Powers, and others almost came to blows with Phoenix players Ricky Sobers and Dennis Awtrey. Meanwhile, in the Boston locker room, coach Tommy Heinsohn almost fainted, requiring medical attention.

The marathon game took an even greater toll on two Suns fans watching on television in Phoenix. Both had to be taken to a hospital when one leaped out of his chair and hit his head on a chandelier. His next door neighbor came rushing over to help but tripped and fell on the way.

Back in Phoenix on Sunday afternoon, the Celtics won Game Six 87–80, to take the series and their thirteenth NBA championship. It was anticlimactic after the unequaled drama of Game Five.

The First Star Center

A basketball powerhouse who devoted fifty years of his life to the game, Joe Lapchick was born in 1900 in Yonkers, New York, just outside New York City. Joe's father had been born in Czechoslovakia and came to the United States at the age of twelve. Times were hard, and when Joe finished grammar school he began working to help his father support their family.

Joe Lapchick made his mark as a player and coach.

One of his jobs was caddying at a nearby golf course, where the golfers included baseball star Christy Mathewson, sportswriter Grantland Rice, and singer Al Jolson. At the age of thirteen, Joe's height was 6′3″, making him a natural candidate for basketball. By the time he was fifteen, he was picking up a few extra bucks playing hoops.

In fact, Joe could earn as much as three dollars for a game, a lot of money at that time. As Joe got better, he was sought by dozens of teams, often playing in up to four of the many different leagues. He resolved his schedule conflicts quite logically: he would play for the team that paid him the most money.

After turning seventeen, Joe was often hired for just one game, to play against the famous Boston Celtics, a rough group of full-grown men, and he paid physically for the privilege. Although 6′5″, Joe was still lanky and awkward, and it was his job to go up against Celtics center Horse Haggerty, a monster of a man at 6′4″ and 240 pounds. Haggerty would batter Joe without letup, leaving him with bruised ribs and arms after every game.

But Lapchick worked hard at the game, concentrating on his footwork, and in 1923, when he was twenty-three years old, the Celtics asked him to join them. Joe was more than happy to sign up with the club for the hefty sum of $50 per game, and eventually replaced Haggerty, becoming the star center on the world's greatest team.

Lapchick played pro ball until 1936, when he became the basketball coach at St. John's University. His teams were very successful, and in 1947 he became the coach of the New York Knicks of the Basketball Association of America, which was the forerunner of the NBA.

In nine years with the Knicks, Lapchick's teams never had a losing season, but the job wore him down, and when St. John's offered him his old job back in 1956, he returned to the campus. Under Joe Lapchick, St. John's won the National Invitation Tournament four times, and twice Lapchick was named the nation's College Coach of the Year.

But it was as a player that Joe Lapchick was elected to the Basketball Hall of Fame in 1966, four years before his death in 1970. And he learned that craft the hard way.

Ideas That Never Quite Caught On

Less than fifteen years after the invention of basketball in 1891, a new form of the game sprung up in the Northeast. It was basketball on roller skates, an early form of "rollerball," you might say, and it had a legion of dedicated participants. Enthusiasm for the new game was so strong that some expected it to replace James Naismith's version of the sport.

At Madison Square Garden in New York in 1906, plans were in the works for a rollerball league, with over fifty teams reportedly expressing interest in joining. But the league was never formed, as the new sport turned out to be just a fad that faded away quickly.

Soon after that came the advent of basketball on horseback, a game that called for some major modifications in the rules. Since players on horseback were much higher off the ground, the free throw line was moved thirty feet from the basket. Dribbling was abolished, and they used a different type of ball that was full of stuffing rather than air, thus making it easier to handle.

Scoring was extremely difficult, as indicated by a game between two military units in New York in 1929, which ended with a score of 9–4. Among the injuries suffered in that game were a broken leg and a spine injury. Not surprisingly, this form of basketball died out quickly as well.

Basketball on ice had a brief fling in the early '30s, most notably a game at the University of Illinois that was captained by two of the school's varsity baseball pitchers. But like baseball on ice (which was popular before the turn of the century), ice basketball slipped from the scene shortly after its arrival.

Some other ill-fated ideas did not alter the playing surface but rather the baskets. The call for higher baskets to help neutralize the big men was heard as far back as 1934, when twelve-foot-high baskets were used in a game between Kansas and Kansas State. After the game, the fans were asked to vote on whether the change should be adopted; 75% of them turned down the higher hoops.

About the same time, the National Association of Basketball Coaches toyed with the idea of enlarging the basket from 18 inches in diameter to 20 inches to improve outside shooting. The University of Missouri served as the guinea pig, using the enlarged hoops from 1936 through '39. But that was the last heard of that idea.

Finally, also in the '30s, a device was invented called a Bask-o-Lite, which had an electric switch across the net. When the ball went through, it turned on a light behind the basket, indicating the successful shot to the spectators. It might have worked in hockey, where they still turn on a goal light to signal the puck entering the goal. But in basketball, the fans had little trouble locating the ball going through the basket, and found the Bask-o-Lite to be an unnecessary extravagance.

Until the red, white, and blue striped basketballs of the ABA in the late 1960s, that was the last of basketball's equipment oddities—which just goes to show how simple a game it really is.

Kareem's Most Remarkable Scoring Streak

As the 1987–88 season began, Kareem Abdul-Jabbar had spent fourteen years in the NBA, averaging 25.9 points a game. In each of his first thirteen seasons, he had led his team in scoring, continuing a streak that had begun in elementary school. But in 1986–87, that streak had ended as Laker teammates Magic Johnson and James Worthy both outscored him.

Still intact, however, was an even more remarkable streak. For ten years, Ka-

Kareem's streak lasted for 10 years.

reem had scored at least 10 points in every game, and even at the age of forty, he seemed likely to continue the streak. He was healthy. And coach Pat Riley had once vowed that the streak would not end while he was coaching the Lakers.

Ironically, the streak came to an end on the same court where it began, at Milwaukee Arena. On October 18, 1977, Abdul-Jabbar had scored just two points in a game when, after being elbowed in the stomach, he reacted angrily with a punch to the head of Bucks center Kent Benson. The punch broke Kareem's right hand and forced him to miss the rest of the game and several more. When he returned, the double-figure streak began.

On December 5, 1987, the Lakers were the defending NBA champions, but they were struggling a bit, and had lost three of their last five games. Abdul-Jabbar was fifth on the team in scoring, and twice he had scored exactly 10 points to keep the streak alive—once requiring overtime to do so. On this night, there would be no overtime to prolong the streak as the Lakers lost 85–83, and Kareem was held to 7 points.

He had gone 787 straight regular season games without being held to a single digit in the scoring column. The end came against Bucks centers Randy Breuer and Paul Mokeski, a pair of seven-footers who were not among the league's elite big men. Kareem took only 10 shots that night, hitting three of them: two sky hooks and a spinning layup to go along with one free throw. He took five shots in the fourth quarter, missing four of them, and had the ball slapped away as he went up for another shot.

When asked his reaction to being the man who stopped Kareem's streak, Breuer replied, "I can't wait to get the Trivial Pursuit game and be asked that question." But the Lakers were not that lighthearted about it.

Abdul-Jabbar quickly left the arena without showering to avoid reporters, but he told a Bucks publicist, "It had to end sometime; that's life. I just wish that we would have won the game." While Kareem was taking it hard, Riley put it all in proper perspective. "I wouldn't make a big deal of the streak ending," he said. "I'm going to toast him for an incredible feat. How many of us score double figures in any game in life?"

And how many of us have done it 787 times in a row?

The Longest Win Streak in Pro Sports History

The NBA's longest winning streak, thirty-three games by the 1971–72 Los Angeles Lakers, is one record that may never be broken. In fact, it's the longest win streak by any major pro sports team in America.

The Lakers that year were an aging team. Elgin Baylor, their captain, was thirty-seven and hobbled by knee injuries. Jerry West was thirty-three. The great Wilt Chamberlain was slowing down at age thirty-five. The Lakers had lost to the Bucks in the playoffs the previous year, prompting the hiring of Bill Sharman as the Lakers' new coach.

Sharman's most important project was motivating his club to play a running game, one keyed by Chamberlain's defense and rebounding. He persuaded Wilt to concentrate on defense and triggering the fast break, convincing the best scorer in history to change his role. Sharman used young Gail Goodrich as his shooting guard, with the veteran West focusing on his defense and playmaking.

Baylor was pulled from the starting lineup, as quick sharpshooter Jim McMillian and defensive ace Happy Hairston started at forward. Baylor retired rather than ride the bench. His retirement served to unify the team as he and Chamberlain had never gotten along. Sharman accepted West's suggestion that Chamberlain be made captain, further motivating Wilt's transformation.

Sharman's strategy worked to perfection. Chamberlain took fewer shots than any Laker starter and scored under 15 points a game. But he led the league in rebounding and field goal percentage. West led the league in assists and scored 25 points a game while Goodrich averaged 26. The Lakers ran up a record of 69–13, the highest winning percentage (.841) in NBA history, and went on to win the championship. They outscored the opposition by an average of 121–109. But most noteworthy about this record season was the winning streak.

It began on November 5, 1971. Just over one month later, on December 10, they tied the league record of twenty straight, which the Milwaukee Bucks had set the previous season. In one of the few close games in the streak, they had to go to overtime to defeat Phoenix at The Forum. The record-breaking twenty-first straight win came two nights later at The Forum in a 104–95 victory over Atlanta.

On December 22, they knocked off the Bullets in Baltimore 127–120. That extended the streak to twenty-seven in a row, breaking the major-league sports record held by baseball's 1916 New York Giants. Amazingly, that Giants team didn't even win the National League pennant, but no such fate awaited the Lakers. They eventually ran the streak to thirty-three consecutive wins when they routed the Hawks 134–90 on January 7, 1972 in Atlanta.

The Lakers finally lost two nights later on January 9 in a nationally televised game against the Bucks, whose record they had totally obliterated. Kareem Abdul-Jabbar piled up 39 points as the Bucks won easily 120–104. But in the playoffs, the Lakers prevailed over the Bucks in the semifinals and the Knicks in the finals, concluding what must be considered the best season in NBA history.

Looking back later on that season, Sharman pointed out, "That team could beat you any way . . . on defense, on offense, on rebounding. Defensively, West had a greater season than any guard I've ever seen, and Wilt did a great job of controlling the middle." And it all came about because Sharman got the Lakers to play the kind of game they were best suited to play—and one they never had before.

The Best-Shooting Big Man in NBA History

One of only five players who has led the NBA in scoring three times, Bob McAdoo helped change the nature of the big man's role in pro basketball. He was one of the first quick, nonphysical centers, when he burst upon the scene in the early '70s. He caused nightmares for opposing defenses. A superb shooter with incredible range, the 6′9″ McAdoo would pull the opposing center away from the basket. If a smaller player tried to guard him, McAdoo would shoot over him.

When McAdoo joined the Buffalo Braves out of the University of North Carolina in 1972, he was forced to play forward against his wishes, as the Braves thought he was too skinny to play the pivot. Despite playing out of position, McAdoo averaged 18 points a game and won the Rookie of the Year Award.

The following year, the Braves traded center Elmore Smith and shifted McAdoo to center. Bob responded with 30.6 points a game to win the NBA scoring title. Although almost half of his shots came from outside, he led the league in field goal percentage. McAdoo lost out to Kareem Abdul-Jabbar in the MVP voting, and he upset some folks by saying that he should have won it. The next year, everyone agreed, as McAdoo led the league with a 34.5 point scoring average and won the MVP Award.

McAdoo was very quick for a big man and had great acceleration to the basket. Although he was criticized for his bad defense, he had great timing and was a good shot blocker. But above all else, McAdoo was a shooter who could hit from anywhere, completely redefining traditional ideas about what was a bad shot.

Bob McAdoo, a big man with range

John Havlicek called him "the best pure shooter I've ever seen." And Billy Cunningham said, "Next to Wilt, he's the greatest scorer I've ever seen."

An unemotional player who always had a dour expression on his face, McAdoo was a center who shot from guard territory. Responding to those who downgraded his defense, Bob replied, "Nobody can score more on me than I can score on them. Not Cowens, not Jabbar, not anybody."

Born in Greensboro, North Carolina, McAdoo led Vincennes Junior College of Indiana to the national junior college championship before transferring to North Carolina. He led the Tar Heels to the Final Four in 1972, where they lost to UCLA, then applied for the NBA hardship draft with a year of eligibility remaining. This caused a furor both in North Carolina and around the NBA.

When McAdoo decided to turn pro, many Tar Heel supporters were irate and made him the target of insults, both written and spoken. Then the Virginia Squires of the ABA informed NBA commissioner Walter Kennedy that McAdoo had already signed with them. Kennedy advised NBA teams not to draft him, a warning that was heeded by the Portland Trailblazers, who had the first pick and selected LaRue Martin of Loyola.

Buffalo picked next and took a chance on McAdoo. It turned out that the Virginia contract was invalid because McAdoo was still a minor. The Braves and

Squires settled the matter out of court, and Buffalo had its new star.

McAdoo went on to play fifteen years in the NBA, and helped the Lakers win two NBA titles as a bench player in the early '80s. He retired with a career scoring average of 22.1, but in his eight years as a starter he averaged over 26 points a game. After leaving the NBA in 1986 at the age of thirty-five, McAdoo headed for Italy where he continued to play pro ball. Italian announcers no doubt came up with their own version of the familiar cry, "That's two for McAdoo!"

Reed's Return Sparks Knicks' First Championship

Entering the 1970 NBA Finals, the New York Knicks were favored to win their first league championship. Red Holzman's team had the league's best record (60–22) during the regular season and had won a record 18 games in a row. With Willis Reed enjoying his best season and Walt Frazier having the first of his All-Star seasons, the Knicks had two 20-point scorers and a supporting cast that included Dick Barnett, Dave DeBusschere, Bill Bradley, and Cazzie Russell.

Like New York, Los Angeles had never won the championship, and this was their twelfth appearance in the Finals. Coached by Joe Mullaney, they had a trio of superstars—Jerry West, Wilt Chamberlain, and Elgin Baylor—and had swept Atlanta in four games in the Western Division Finals.

The two teams split the first four games of the Championship Series, with two of them going into overtime. Then, in Game Five, the Knicks pulled out a 107–100 win in New York, but lost Reed during the game with a torn thigh muscle. Lacking a strong backup center, the Knicks appeared to have little chance without Reed occupying Chamberlain. That feeling was proven true in Game Six at Los Angeles. Reed was unable to play, Chamberlain went wild, and the Lakers won by 22 points.

It appeared unlikely that Reed would be ready for Game Seven two days later, but no one knew for sure as he took a variety of injections. Without him, the Knicks might as well not show up. Even a partially healthy Reed might give them a chance.

Two hours before the game, Reed went onto the court at Madison Square Garden. He tested his injured leg, but he was still unsure if he could play. When the teams took the court for pregame warm-ups, Reed was nowhere to be seen, and worried Knicks fans were expecting the worst. Then, just five minutes before game time, Reed limped onto the court to a thundering ovation. He took a few shots, grimacing in pain, and went to the bench.

When the starting lineups were announced moments later, Reed's name was called, and the Garden went berserk. The Lakers won the opening tip but missed their first shot, and the Knicks got the ball. Frazier fed Reed at the top of the key, and Willis sank a jumper that lit up the Garden again. A minute later, Reed pulled down a defensive rebound, and when the Knicks came down court he sank another twenty-footer. Sparked by his presence, the Knicks ripped the game open, jumping to a 15–6 lead.

Although Reed never scored another point, the Knicks opened an insurmountable halftime lead of 69–42 as Frazier poured in 23 points. Reed finished the game with just 4 points and 3 rebounds, but the twenty-seven painful minutes he played were the key to victory. The final score was 113–99, with Frazier racking up 36 points and 19 assists and DeBusschere pulling down 17 rebounds.

Reed was selected as the series MVP and admitted afterward that even with injections of painkillers, he doubted his ability to play that night. "I didn't even think I could walk out there," he said. "But this was the championship. I couldn't sit on the bench and watch it. I had to do what I could."

Reed completed a rare hat trick that year, winning the MVP Award in the regular season, the All-Star Game, and the Championship Series. His mere presence on the court for Game Seven proved him worthy of even more honors than those, and meant a championship for New York.

The Backboard Busters

When one thinks of the sight of a glass backboard shattering, with fragments flying everywhere, naturally it's the flamboyant Darryl Dawkins that comes to mind. While playing for Philadelphia in 1979, Dawkins smashed two backboards in less than a month, and the replays have been shown thousands of times since then.

Darryl Dawkins

Chuck Connors, before his "Rifleman" days

Dawkins's first backboard demolition, at Kansas City's Municipal Auditorium, was preserved for eternity in Darryl's own words as the "Chocolate-Thunder-Flying, Robinzine-Crying, Teeth-Shaking, Glass-Breaking, Rump-Roasting, Bun-Toasting, Wham-Bam, Glass-Breaker-I-Am Jam." The game was delayed for an hour and ten minutes, as maintenance workers picked up glass fragments as far away as midcourt and an old basket standard was wheeled out of the basement.

Dawkins' backboard explosions led to the use of the "toss-back" rim, which snaps down with excessive pressure. NBA Commissioner Larry O'Brien also instituted stiff punishment for future offenders, including a fine, a technical foul, ejection from the game, and suspension from the following game.

Thanks to today's sharing of NBA highlights by TV stations around the country, Dawkins is the man who became famous for exploding backboards. But he was by no means the first to do it in the pros.

In the '60s, the Baltimore Bullets had a high-flying forward named Gus Johnson who introduced the whirling dunks that "Dr. J," Julius Erving, would make famous. NBA coach Dick Motta once said, "Gus Johnson was 'Dr. J' before Julius ever thought of being Dr. J."

Well, it seems that Gus had some Darryl Dawkins in him, too. As a rookie in 1963, he shattered a backboard in a game at Oakland. He repeated the feat in 1965 at St. Louis and again at Milwaukee in 1971.

But Johnson was not the first of the backboard busters, either. That distinction belongs to none other than Chuck Connors—yes, "the Rifleman" himself. As a second-year pro out of Seton Hall in 1946, 6'7" Connors was a member of the Boston Celtics. On the night the Celtics and Chicago Stags were opening the Boston Arena for pro ball, Connors went up for a layup during warm-ups and grabbed the rim. The glass backboard broke into hundreds of pieces, and it took two hours to replace the backboard with one from the Boston Garden across town.

Connors' NBA career lasted only 67 games over three seasons, as he averaged only 4 points a game. He then turned his attention to baseball, and also played in exactly 67 big-league games in that sport. As a first baseman with the Dodgers in 1949 and the Cubs in 1951, Connors hit a combined .238 with 2 home runs in 201 at bats. Chuck then went on to greater fame and fortune in Hollywood, but he had already demonstrated a flair for the theatrical as the first of pro basketball's backboard busters.

The Misunderstanding That Created a Sport

The first women's basketball game was played just a few weeks after the first game played by James Naismith's men's class in 1891 in Springfield, Massachusetts. Some grade-school teachers asked Naismith if it would be all right for them to play, and he had no objection. The women showed up in their street clothes, most of them wearing their regular shoes, although some wore tennis shoes.

Everyone survived, and the game had one interesting long-lasting byproduct. One of the women, Maude Sherman, went on to marry Dr. Naismith.

The first women's collegiate game was played at nearby Smith College in Northampton, Massachusetts, in 1893. Physical education director Sendra Bernsen, who had learned about the game while attending a seminar in New Haven, arranged a game between her freshmen and sophomore classes. Male spectators were banned from the gym to prevent them from seeing the bloomers worn by the players.

These early women's games were played under Naismith's standard rules, a practice that began to change in 1895. Clara Baer, a physical education teacher at

Newcomb College in New Orleans, wrote a letter to James Naismith asking for a copy of his basketball rules. Naismith's reply included a diagram of the court that pointed out the positions where the players usually were stationed. Baer misunderstood, believing that the players were not allowed to leave their specific areas.

Baer's misinterpretation gave birth to the women's rules that prevailed for more than seventy years in most of North America—the game in which players had to stay within defined areas and only a few players on each team could shoot.

Baer called the game Basquette and later defended the restrictions on movement, stating that basketball had to be changed for the "use of women and growing girls; a game where a delicate girl, unaccustomed to exercise, and for the most part averse to it, would become interested in spite of herself."

Most physical education instructors at the time agreed with that philosophy, and believed that women would be physically endangered if the court did not have specific division lines that players could not cross. Baer's rules became accepted nationwide, and it took the better part of a century for women athletes to shake off the chains that had restricted them as a result of Naismith's diagram being misunderstood. The woman's game now, of course, is identical to men's basketball in almost every respect, and often just as exciting.

Seattle U Shocks the Globetrotters

One of basketball's greatest upsets occurred on January 21, 1952. A special game was played that night to raise money for the United States Olympic Games Fund, matching the Seattle University Chieftains against the Harlem Globetrotters.

Under coach Al Brightman, the Chieftains were led by the O'Brien twins, Johnny and Ed, who had received the first full four-year basketball scholarships in the school's history. Johnny O'Brien was the top scorer in the nation, but fans doubted he could hurt the Globetrotters, because Johnny and Ed O'Brien were each all of 5′9″ tall. And the Chieftains' tallest player, Bill Higlin, was only 6′4″.

The Globetrotters had played over 3,500 games in their history, winning almost ninety-four percent of them. Usually they would open a big lead before going into their crowd-pleasing routines. On this night, they were without their ballhandling wizard Marques Haynes, who had to appear at his draft board, but the rest of their squad was intact.

To make the game as big a fund-raiser as possible, both teams paid their own expenses. And the University of Washington donated the use of its athletic pavilion, which had 11,500 seats.

At least 13,000 fans poured into the building before the fire department closed the doors. Entertainer Louis Armstrong was there to perform at halftime, even though he was giving a concert later that evening. The stage was set for a wild night, and that's just what it was.

Seattle established early that they would not be an easy mark. They quickly jumped out to a 22–15 lead with Johnny O'Brien scoring 16 points, despite being guarded by the Globetrotters' star, "Goose" Tatum. The Globetrotters were missing their shots, and when Ed O'Brien sank a thirty-footer at the half-time buzzer, Seattle led 46–36. Louis Armstrong was so swept up in the excitement that he stayed for the second half, missing his scheduled show downtown.

Early in the third quarter, the Globetrotters rallied to tie it 53–53. Late in the quarter, Johnny O'Brien had to leave with a sprained ankle. But his teammates regained the lead, 65–59, as the third-quarter buzzer sounded.

Johnny O'Brien returned for the fourth quarter with his ankle taped, and the teams traded baskets down the stretch. With nine seconds left, a jump ball was called with Seattle leading by 2 points. The Trotters wanted a time-out. Referee Pop Hagerty informed them that they were out of time-outs, but could have one in exchange for a technical foul against them. They insisted on the time-out, and Johnny O'Brien hit the technical free throw to put Seattle up by three. Time ran out without another shot being taken, and the Chieftains had pulled off the upset.

An elated crowd flooded the court as the scoreboard showed the final score: Seattle 84, Globetrotters 81. The 5′9″ Johnny O'Brien, guarded by the great Goose Tatum much of the game, had scored 43 points.

After college basketball, the O'Briens tried pro baseball.

Bibliographical Note

Among the source materials used in researching this book, I found the following to be indispensable: *The NBA's Official Encyclopedia of Pro Basketball,* edited by Zander Hollander; *All The Moves,* by Neil D. Isaacs; *The Cavalcade of Basketball,* by Alexander M. Weyand; *50 Years of Basketball,* by Joe Lapchick; *Basketball's Hall of Fame,* by Sandy Padwe; *24 Seconds to Shoot,* by Leonard Koppett; *The Complete Book of Basketball: A New York Times Scrapbook History; Basketball's Greatest Teams,* by Al Hirshberg; and *Basketball's Greatest Games,* edited by Zander Hollander.

Also helpful were the following:

Basketball: Its Origin and Development, by James Naismith; *Mr. Basketball—George Mikan's Own Story,* as told to Bill Carlson; *God, Man and Basketball Jones,* by Charles Rosen; *Hondo, Celtic Man in Motion,* by John Havlicek and Bob Ryan; *Second Wind,* by Bill Russell and Taylor Branch; *Parting Shots,* by Dan Issel with Buddy Martin; *505 Basketball Questions Your Friends Can't Answer,* by Sol Barzman; *The Franklin Wonder Five,* by Phillip Ellett; *From Set Shot to Slam Dunk,* by Charles Salzberg; *The Amazing Basketball Book—The First 100 Years,* by Bob Hill and Randall Brown; *The Lonely Heroes: Professional Basketball's Great Centers,* by Merv Harris; *They Were Number One,* by Robert Stern; *The Essence of the Game Is Deception,* by Leonard Koppett; *Playoff!,* by Dave Klein; *Strange but True Basketball Stories,* by Howard Liss; *Pro Basketball: Its Superstars and History,* edited by Zander Hollander; *Great Rookies of Pro Basketball,* compiled by Zander Hollander; *Harlem Globetrotters,* by George Vecsey; *One on One,* by Jim Bukata; *Basketball Stars of 1970, 1972, 1973,* by Louis Sabin; *Basketball Stars of 1968, 1969,* by Berry Stainback; *Basketball Stars of 1974,* by Hal Bock and Ben Olan; *Pro Basketball Superstars of 1975,* by Bruce Lowitt and Bert Rosenthal; *Sports Firsts,* by Patrick Clark; *The Great American Sports Book,* by George Gipe.

Extensive use was also made of *The New York Times, Sports Illustrated, The New York Post,* and numerous other newspapers and periodicals.

Photo Credits

Cover, Golden State Warriors; p. 4, Golden State Warriors; p. 7, Hickox Library at the Naismith Memorial Basketball Hall of Fame; p. 9, University of San Francisco; p. 12, Hall of Fame; p. 15, UCLA; p. 18, United Press International; p. 21, Hall of Fame; p. 23, Topps Chewing Gum, Inc. Courtesy of First Base Baseball Card Shop, Dallas, Texas; p. 26, Hall of Fame; p. 28, Hall of Fame; p. 31, Hall of Fame; p. 34, Hall of Fame; p. 37, Hall of Fame; p. 39, Hall of Fame; p. 41, Hall of Fame; p. 44, Hall of Fame; p. 47, Boston Celtics; p. 49, University of Houston; p. 50, University of Houston; p. 53, Hall of Fame; p. 56, Hall of Fame; p. 58, Hall of Fame; p. 61, Detroit Pistons; p. 64, Hall of Fame; p. 67, Hall of Fame; p. 69, Hall of Fame; p. 72, Hall of Fame; p. 75, Hall of Fame; p. 77, UCLA; p. 80, Hall of Fame; p. 82, Hall of Fame; p. 85, Topps, Courtesy of First Base; p. 87, University of Wisconsin; p. 89, Hall of Fame; p. 92, Hall of Fame; p. 95, Texas Sports Hall of Fame Foundation; p. 98, Hall of Fame; p. 101, Hall of Fame; p. 103, University of Utah; p. 106, Utah Jazz; p. 109, Furman University; p. 111, Hall of Fame; p. 115, Duke University; p. 118, University of Southern California; p. 120, Hall of Fame; p. 123, UCLA; p. 124, UCLA; p. 127, Hall of Fame; p. 129, Hall of Fame; p. 132, Topps, Courtesy of First Base; p. 135, Purdue University; p. 137, Hall of Fame; p. 140, Hall of Fame; p. 142, Topps, Courtesy of First Base; p. 145, UCLA; p. 148, Hall of Fame; p. 153, University of San Francisco; p. 155, Houston Rockets; p. 159, Hall of Fame; p. 161, Hall of Fame; p. 164, Associated Press; p. 167, Topps, Courtesy of First Base; p. 169, Topps, Courtesy of First Base; p. 170, Hall of Fame; p. 173, Topps, Courtesy of First Base.

INDEX